The Valley

of the

Son

*Fulfilling Christ's Redemptive Purpose
for Greater Phoenix
in the 21st Century*

Robert J. Winters

Restoration International Ministries
and Publications, Inc.

Unless otherwise indicated, all Scripture quotations are taken from the *New King James Version* of the Bible.

The Valley of the Son - Fulfilling Christ's Redemptive Purpose for Greater Phoenix in the 21st Century

Published by:
Restoration International Ministries and Publications, Inc.
3914 W. Hackamore Drive
Glendale, Arizona 85310
(623) 581-0731

International Standard Book Number 0-9675907-0-1

Printed in the United States of America.

Dedication

To the church in the Valley of the Sun, who has been sovereignly mobilized at this strategic time in history, to fulfill the Lord's redemptive calling on Phoenix to be a city of refuge, restoration, and revival for multitudes.

Acknowledgments

I would like to thank Theresa Walker and Jeffrey Cuellar for contributing key historical information on Greater Phoenix which supports the spiritual insights communicated in this book.

I would also like to thank Claire Lopeman, Joan Miller, Jen Hughes, Chuck Jackson and Leigh Jackson for editing and commenting on the final manuscript.

I especially want to thank my wife Kay and my children for their patience and understanding through the time consuming book writing process.

Preface

My motivation for writing this book was birthed from a personal commission from the Lord. In the Fall of 1995, after eight years of fruitful labor in Charleston, South Carolina, my wife Kay and I had sensed that our work there was completed. I had written the book, *"Reviving the Holy City - Christ's Challenge Concerning the Church in Charleston"* in 1994, and had completed a year long series of meetings throughout the city wherein I had preached repentance, prophesied restoration and promoted revival. We knew that the Lord was preparing us for a major move, yet we didn't have any specifics as to exactly where He was directing us. We committed this matter to the Lord in prayer, and simply agreed that we would move anywhere the Lord directed.

On December 19, 1995 the Lord awakened me in the middle of the night. As I sat in our kitchen sensing His presence, the following words came to me, "Where you are moving you have visited before. You are moving to Phoenix, AZ." I had remembered that 3 years prior I had a one day business trip to Phoenix. During that brief visit, I thoroughly enjoyed Phoenix and had jokingly suggested to Kay over the phone that we might move there someday. After that short conversation, nothing more had ever been said about Phoenix.

The following day, as I was coming home from work, I was apprehensive in sharing with Kay what the Lord had revealed to me the night before concerning our move to Phoenix. Kay's entire immediate family resided in a small rural town in Georgia, and I knew she was hoping that the Lord would keep us in the Southeastern part of the United States. That night I said to her, "I believe the Lord showed me last night where we are to move, and you're not going to like it." Before I said another word, Kay blurted out, "Phoenix!" Dumbfounded, I replied, "How did you know that?" She said, "The Lord woke me up last night and showed me we are to move there." That was all the confirmation that we needed.

Before our cross-country move to Phoenix in April of 1996, the Lord revealed to me on March 28 one of the primary purposes for Him moving us to Phoenix. Our mission entailed proclaiming Greater Phoenix's divine redemptive purpose as a city of refuge, and helping prepare the Church in the Valley of the Sun to minister to a massive influx of lost and hurting people that would overwhelm the city in the early 21st century. The Lord impressed upon me that I was to spearhead this mission through a book I was to author and entitle, *"The Valley of the Son"*.

After two years in the Phoenix area, the Lord released me in May of 1998 to commence writing the book that you are about to read. May the Lord enlighten, inspire and challenge you through the following pages. For indeed, the Sun of Righteousness shall arise to minister healing and hope to the multitudes that continue to migrate to the Valley of the Sun in search of regeneration, refuge, and restoration.

Robert J. Winters
Restoration International Ministries and Publications, Inc.
Glendale, Arizona

Table of Contents

Section II - Defeating Demonic Deterrents to Greater Phoenix's Divine Destiny

Introduction

Prophetic vision formulates destiny, and destiny supplies purpose. Without a vision, people perish (Proverbs 29:18). Without a sense of destiny and a meaningful purpose, life is reduced to an aimless and fruitless existence that is often governed by men's lusts instead of God's will. Unfortunately, millions of unbelievers and Christians alike live their entire lives in this manner.

However, before time began, the Lord Jesus Christ, according to His own purpose and grace, called each and every one of us with a holy calling (II Timothy 1:9). Heavenly callings can be birthed through a prophetic word, vision, dream, divine revelation, angelic visitation, or more simply through a Holy Spirit inspired desire, idea, or motivation. Although divine destinies and heavenly callings are irrevocable, they never fully manifest without the cooperation of God's people (Romans 11:29).

The gifts and calling of God are not restricted in scope to individuals, but span entire people groups, including cities and nations (Joshua 20). Divine callings upon cities and nations are more complex and crucial than those upon individual lives. Until now, the purposes of God for cities and nations have for the most part remained hidden from mankind. However, as the Lord's end-time strategies for global harvest unfold before the Church, specific direction will be given by the Lord concerning each city's and nation's redemptive role and purpose in accomplishing the Master's plan.

The Church is the primary element through which the Lord establishes His kingdom and fulfills His divine purpose in cities. Therefore, it is the responsibility of the spiritual leadership or the "elders at the gate" of each city to collectively seek the heart of God to discover and participate in His plan for taking their city for the Lord Jesus Christ.

Phoenix is currently the sixth largest city and Maricopa County the fastest growing county in the United States. When God begins to gather people into a city at a phenomenal rate, one can be sure that He is about to do something glorious. Such is the case with the Valley of the Sun.

I believe that the Lord Jesus Christ has commissioned me to write this prophetic revelation as a trumpet sound to the Church in the Phoenix area, that we might more fully comprehend our mission, and be inspired and equipped to fulfill our heavenly calling as a city of refuge to multitudes in the 21st century.

Section I

Discovering Christ's Redemptive Purpose for Greater Phoenix

Chapter 1

Phoenix's First Flight

Discovering identity precedes the perception of divine destiny. Without knowing who we are, from where we have come and what we have already accomplished, it is difficult if not impossible to discern our ultimate destiny in God. This principle applies to individuals as well as cities.

To facilitate our comprehension of Phoenix's heavenly calling and redemptive purpose, it is crucial that we commence our search for Phoenix's identity as far back in time as possible. Without a clear understanding of our past, our vision for the future is dimmed.

> Habakkuk 2:2 "Write the vision and make it plain on tablets, that he may run who reads it. For the vision is yet for an appointed time; but at the end it will speak, and it will not lie. Though it tarries, wait for it. Because it will surely come, it will not tarry."

This book is not intended to be predominantly historical in nature. However, significant historical events, patterns, and themes, will be identified, including characteristics of key people from Phoenix's past and present, so that the divine destiny of the Valley of the Sun can be clearly defined. In addition, hindrances to the fulfillment of the Phoenix's heavenly calling will also be identified, that we might through Christ remove them, and press on to fulfill our corporate heavenly calling (Philippians 3:14).

Although the phoenix's significance in defining the redemptive calling upon the Valley of the Sun will be discussed in greater detail in Chapter 3, the following brief exposé of the mythological phoenix will facilitate one's understanding of Chapters 1 and 2.

The phoenix was a fabled bird in Greek mythology. Only one such bird existed at any time, and it was always male. It had brilliant gold and reddish-purple feathers and was as large or larger than the eagle. According to most Greek writers, the phoenix lived between 300 and 500 years. At the end of each life cycle, the phoenix burned itself on a funeral pyre. Another phoenix then arose from the ashes with renewed youth and beauty. The long life of the phoenix and its dramatic rebirth from its own ashes, made it a symbol of immortality and spiritual rebirth.[1]

Our Hohokam Heritage

The Hohokam culture of American Indians inhabited modern day Phoenix from approximately 300 B.C. to 1450 A.D. Their culture has been divided into four distinct developmental periods: the Pioneer period (300 B.C. to A.D. 550), the Colonial period (550-900), the Sedentary period (900-1100), and the Classic period (1100-1450).[2] Although these periods mark major changes in Hohokam building architecture, ceramics and architecture, attention will be given to unique cultural characteristics from which redemptive purpose can be prophetically extracted.

Our Water Is Our Future

The Hohokam ingeniously designed and built an intricate network of canals, sourced primarily from the Salt River and Gila River Valley basins, that watered fields of corn, barley, cotton and other crops. The success of their entire economy was based on the integrity of their irrigation system, whose canals totaled a distance of over 300 miles.[3] Ironically, one of Phoenix's mottos, "Our Water is Our Future" had its origins with the Hohokam culture.

Water is a symbol of life, both in the natural and in the spirit realm. Arizona, an Indian word meaning "place of small springs", was foreordained by God to become a refreshing fountain of life to those who thirst not only physically but spiritually.[4]

> Isaiah 35:6,7 "For waters shall burst forth in the wilderness, and streams in the desert. The parched ground shall become a pool, and the thirsty land springs of water."

Prophetically speaking, even as the Hohokam successfully transformed the Sonoran desert into an oasis, Jehovah has destined the Valley of the Sun to become a spring of eternal life to millions. In other words, the Lord fully intends for Greater Phoenix to evolve into a hub for mass evangelism.

> John 4:14 "Whoever drinks of the water that I shall give him will never thirst. But the water that I shall give him will become in him a fountain of water springing up into everlasting life."

Water is also a symbol for the flowing of the Holy Spirit. The key to the Hohokam's success was not the water in and of itself, but their labor in excavating and building miles of trenches and canals that enabled the water to flow to the land and people.

> John 7:37-39 "If anyone thirsts, let him come and drink. He who believes in Me, as the Scripture has said, out of his heart will flow rivers of living water. But this He spoke concerning the Spirit, whom those believing in Him would receive."

17

In a spiritual context, water must flow for it to minister life. For example, it was only when an angel of the Lord stirred up the water in Pool of Bethesda that healing virtue manifested (John 5:4).

It is interesting to note that the Hohokam's canals "spread out like the roots of a tree", delivering water to tens of thousands of acres of dry land.[5] When roots or branches are separated from a tree, they wither, die, and are useless. Similarly, when believers and churches isolate themselves from the rest of the Body, they wither and die spiritually.

Proverbs 18:1 "A man who isolates himself seeks his own desire; he rages against all wise judgment."

Figuratively speaking, the Lord desires us, like the Hohokam, to dig trenches to others in the Body of Christ, that we might supply the life giving water of the Holy Spirit to one another.

Make This Valley Full of Canals

Using only sharp rock axes and wooden sticks, the Hohokam dug several miles of canals throughout the Valley of the Sun. Emil Haury, a 20th century Hohokam scholar noted, "No Indian achievement north of Mexico, in pre-Conquest times, surpassed the Hohokam canal system for planning, expenditure of effort, and for the evident intercommunity organization that produced it."[6] How then shall we replicate the Hohokam's accomplishment in a spiritual context? An Old Testament account provides a practical answer to this question.

In the second book of Kings, through the prophet Elisha, the Lord promised the parched kings and people of Israel, Judah and Edom an abundant supply of water and victory over the Moabites if they would simply make the wilderness valley they were in full of canals.

II Kings 3:16-18   And Elisha said, "Thus says the Lord: **'Make this valley full of canals.'** For thus says the Lord: 'You shall not see wind, nor shall you see rain; yet that valley shall be filled with water, so that you, your cattle, and your animals may drink.' And this is but a trivial thing in the sight of the Lord; He will also deliver the Moabites into your hand."

In the natural, this command from the Lord seems absurd. However, closer examination of this passage reveals that the Lord's promise of flooding the valley would be accomplished neither through man's efforts nor by any visible natural means. Notice that it was only when a sacrifice was made that the water suddenly flooded the valley.

II Kings 3:20   "Now it happened in the morning, **when the grain offering was offered, that suddenly water came by way of Edom,** and the land was filled with water."

Edom, from which the water came, means "red", and speaks of the blood of Jesus that was shed through His sacrifice on the cross. Prophetically speaking, the flood of revival waters will only come to the Valley of the Sun as our spiritual kings make the consecrated sacrifice of uniting in the Spirit. The Lord will then command the blessing of true revival leading to community transformation (Psalm 133).

Practically speaking, we must expand our vision beyond that of our local churches and ministries, subordinate our private agendas to God's corporate purpose, and make a passionate effort to covenant in the Spirit with the Body of Christ throughout Greater Phoenix. Neither one church, nor one denomination can accomplish by themselves what God can perform supernaturally through our obedience to walk as one. As the unity of the Spirit is realized in our

19

Valley, we will not only collectively discern and defeat the demonic strongholds that deter an open heavens, but also comprehend and consummate the redemptive purpose and eternal plan of God for the Valley of the Sun (Ephesians 4:1-3).

The Washing of Water

In Scripture, water also symbolizes the cleansing and sanctifying effect that the word of God has on the Body of Christ.

> Ephesians 5:26   "That He (Christ) might sanctify and cleanse it (the Church) with the washing of water by the word, that He might present it to Himself a glorious church."

As we allow the river of God to flow to one another, the water of the preached and taught word of God will cleanse and heal the wounds of the past and set us apart as a holy and glorious church.

Like the Hohokam, if we determine to dig channels to one another so that the life giving water of the Spirit freely flows, the Valley of the Sun will evolve into one of the greatest conference and teaching centers in the United States. As the word of the Lord is brought forth and embraced, the Body of Christ in greater Phoenix shall prosper and bring forth much fruit in due season.

> Psalm 1:2,3   "His delight is in the law of the Lord, and in His law he meditates day and night. He shall be like a tree planted by the channels of water, that brings forth its fruit in its season, whose leaf also shall not wither; and whatever he does shall prosper."

In 1989, Rick Joyner, prophet and editor of *The Morning Star Journal*, had a vision of twelve cities in the United States that were destined to become centers for annual conferences to which the Church at large would flock to be fully equipped for the work of the Lord. Each of these twelve cities would have an important and unique message to impart. These conferences would facilitate the strengthening of interdenominational relationships that are necessary in promoting the unity of the Spirit. Phoenix was one of these twelve cities.[7]

Founded in 1981, the BridgeBuilders International Leadership Network, led by Hal and Cheryl Sacks, have annually conducted the Greater Phoenix Pastors and Leaders Prayer Summit since 1989 in an effort to unite and network pastors and church leaders of all Christian denominations throughout the Valley of the Sun. This strategic prayer and worship event is tailored to create a venue in which trust is built between pastors and church leaders. The resultant unity of the Spirit and trust imparted among Phoenician pastors and church leaders is trickling down into their congregations and is providing a firm foundation for community transformation. In 1999, BridgeBuilders International Leadership Network facilitated the birth of the Pastor's Prayer Network for the purpose of giving leadership to the pastors prayer movement of Greater Phoenix. As a result, numerous weekly pastors prayer cells throughout Greater Phoenix have been planted, where pastors are not only praying together, but working cooperatively to reach their communities with the Gospel. One of the prayer cells includes some thirty pastors, which bring their churches together monthly for corporate prayer.

Of the annual conferences held here in the Valley of the Sun, Phoenix First Assembly of God's Annual Pastor's and Leaders School has probably had the greatest impact on the largest number of Church leaders. Since 1977, Pas-

tor Tommy Barnett has inspired and encouraged thousands
of pastors and Church leaders from all over America to
press toward the mark for the prize of fulfilling their high
calling to the glory of God. Tommy Barnett has been a
forerunner in propagating Phoenix's unique message and
ministry to America, which is one of hope that rekindles
the flame of deferred divine dreams, restores clear vision
and prophetic purpose, and inspires the pursuit of heavenly
callings.

Good Roots Yield Much Fruit

Unique to the Hohokam culture was the quantity
and variety of fruit that was brought forth from the fields.
The Hohokam, despite the harsh desert conditions, were
able to reap mass amounts of at least sixteen species of
cultivated plants.[8] The Hohokam's tree-like network of canals and trenches was the secret to their abundant harvest.

In like manner, as the roots of the Church in Greater
Phoenix break through denominational, racial, and cultural
barriers, our branches will grow and extend beyond our local churches, yielding a plenteous and variegated spiritual
harvest.

However, this tree of life will not grow on its own,
but will require our persistent pursuit to promote the unity
of the Spirit in the bond of peace. This work will require
skilled ditch diggers, who are anointed and willing to pay a
spiritual price to see the water of life flow to all parts of the
Valley of the Sun.

Planting Our Best Seeds

During the Hohokam period, different strains of
crops were not hardy enough to withstand the droughts and
freezing temperatures. Year after year, the best seeds were

saved and passed on, resulting in a progressively healthy and robust crop.[9]

Similarly, those pastors and leaders, who have weathered spiritual droughts and withstood adversity only to thrive and bring forth spiritual fruit year after year, must lead the Body of Christ in the Valley of the Sun into the move of God coming in the 21st century. In addition to their cultivated wisdom and zeal, these spiritual leaders must also be willing to sacrifice, at least in part, their private pursuit of a prosperous local church in favor of a kingdom-minded endeavor of building a unified city Church.

> John 12:24 "Most assuredly, I say to you, unless a grain of wheat falls into the ground and dies, it remains alone; but if it dies, it produces much fruit."

Many Phoenician pastors, leaders, intercessors, and churches in the recent past, who have valiantly attempted to promote unity and revival here, have fallen short of their goal and suffered Satan's retaliation. Nevertheless, the commencement of the 21st century will mark the beginning of the end of Satan's dominion over the Valley of the Sun. For truly the Phoenician Church shall arise from the ashes of failure, and fulfill its destiny by transforming Greater Phoenix into a city of refuge for thousands of lost and hurting people.

Chapter 2

The Funeral of the First Phoenix

Although the Hohokam thrived in the Valley of the Sun for several hundred years, they abandoned the Salt and Gila River Valleys around the year 1398 A.D.[1] By 1450 A.D. the Hohokam culture disintegrated and virtually disappeared.[2] An understanding of the contributing factors that brought about their demise establishes a foundation for uncovering historical societal patterns. These patterns not only contribute to defining our corporate redemptive purpose, but also assist us in identifying the spiritual strongholds that have hindered the fulfillment of Greater Phoenix's unique, heavenly calling.

In the previous chapter, it was discovered that the future of the Hohokam culture was dependent upon their unique network of canals which supplied water to their people and lands. In like manner, the spiritual future of the Valley of the Sun depends upon the Greater Phoenician Church corporately making a sacrifice to unite in the Spirit. For only then can the Lord flood our Valley with the life giving waters of revival.

Examining the Ashes

Another unique characteristic of the Hohokam was their cremation of the dead, which was uncommon among other Indian cultures such as the Pima, Anasazi, and Mogollon. Offerings of the finest pottery, stone palettes, shell jewelry, pyrite mirrors, and tools were placed with each body in the funeral pyre, and the residual ashes were buried in several different locations.[3] Mourning rites of their religion called for them to burn the personal property of the deceased on the anniversary of the death.[4] The largest funerals were given for teenagers who had died.[5]

At the very least, it can be surmised that the Hohokam highly esteemed human life, especially budding youth who would determine the future of the Hohokam culture. Some contend that the Hohokam believed there was a release of life through cremation.[6] Interestingly enough, this notion is analogous to the birth and emergence of the Phoenix from the funeral pyre of its predecessor. The theme of new life and restoration appears throughout the history of the Valley of the Sun and supports the premise that Greater Phoenix is ordained by God to be a center for birthing and restoring divine dreams.

Walls of Isolation

The Hohokam rarely chose to congregate in tight-knit communities. They built simple houses and kept a respectable distance from their neighbors. Snaketown, just south of Phoenix, serves as a prime example of this practice, as approximately 1000 inhabitants were spread out over 400 acres of land. Emil Haury, an expert on the Hohokam, while excavating Snaketown in 1964, noted that the spacious layout of the village suggested that the Hohokam believed that "close spacing of houses was not the key to quality living".[7] Interestingly enough, modern Phoenix has adopted the same philosophy, as we have one of the lowest population densities of any major city in America today. We have grown apart and not together.

During the Hohokam Classic Period, entire villages were enclosed by walls that created compounds. These walls seemed to direct or limit access to certain parts of the village.[8] If one observes Greater Phoenix today, houses and buildings are predominantly separated by walls. This structural pattern is more than just a coincidence, but characterizes a spiritual stronghold that victimizes Phoenicians through isolation. The Hohokam and Phoenician tendency to isolate themselves does not stem from social preference, but is the result of a demonic tactic that serves to thwart the consummation of divine destinies.

The Body of Christ is a living spiritual organism that requires the active participation of every member if we are to succeed in actualizing God's corporate purposes in the earth (I Corinthians 12:12-27). The fulfillment of our personal heavenly calling does not solely depend on our individual efforts, but also on the integral response of those around us. When we isolate ourselves or reject those whom God has placed in our lives, we not only hinder the fulfillment of our heavenly calling, but also impede others in the Body from functioning at full capacity.

Isolation is one predominant, visible effect of Satan's onslaught against believers and non-believers alike in the Valley of the Sun. An in-depth examination reveals some root causes of isolation.

The Seed of Destruction

During the Classic Period (1100 A.D. - 1450 A.D.), the final era of the Hohokam culture, platform mounds that resembled unfinished pyramids were constructed at three mile intervals along the Salt and Gila Rivers. The platform mounds had several rooms that were enclosed by massive adobe walls, which gave the impression that only the privileged could enter.[9]

Frank Hamilton Cushing, an archeologist from the 1880s, suggested that the platform mounds reflected some sort of hierarchy. He thought that the Hohokam elite and their families lived in the mounds, while the great unwashed majority entered only by special permission. The Hohokam culture apparently had evolved from a cooperative fellowship into a society of "haves" and "have nots", where an upper-class priesthood lorded over the affairs of the common folk. Cushing's views have recently been reinforced by in-depth investigations of the mounds.[10]

Pride is the most powerful seed of Satan, a spiritual disease whose end is always destruction. When pride is planted into the hearts of mankind, they presumptuously exalt themselves above others.

Proverbs 16:18 "Pride goes before destruction, and a haughty spirit before a fall."

Elitism is the fruit borne from a heart that has been tainted by pride. The most prevalent form of elitism is racism, which is a common thread interwoven throughout the fabric of the Valley of the Sun's history. One dominant manifestation of an elitist attitude is the rejection of those who do not measure up to predetermined standards, resulting in their estrangement and isolation.

Throughout the Colonial (550 A.D. - 900 A.D.) and Sedentary (900 A.D. - 1100 A.D.) periods, the Hohokam successfully combated elitism by engaging in ceremonial ball games that served to unite Hohokam heartland communities to their neighbors up and down the rivers. By 1980, 193 "ball courts" were found at 154 sites, ranging from as far north as Flagstaff to south of Tucson. Forty percent of these were in the Phoenix basin, along the Gila and Salt Rivers.[11]

Like modern day sporting events, the Hohokam ball games served to strengthen relationships and improve communication among the various villages. Community interaction helps dissolve the prejudices and biases that foster elitism. Unfortunately, the rise of elitism among the Hohokam at the advent of the Classic Period (1100 A.D. - 1450 A.D.) resulted in a breakdown of inter-tribal communication and trust, evidenced by the gradual disappearance of the ball court games.[12]

Internal Strife Led to External Oppression

As elitist attitudes increased among the Hohokam, they became divided. In addition, extended periods of drought (1325 A.D. - 1357 A.D.) and flooding (1358 A.D.) proved to be catastrophic to the land and people.[13] The cycle of droughts and floods destroyed irrigation canals which adversely impacted the food supply. Along with these unfavorable climatic effects, the migration of the Salado and Sinagua Indians from the north into the Hohokam villages placed an additional burden on the Hohokam.[14]

History demonstrates that under the most adverse conditions, a united people can overcome the most grave of circumstances. However, a people divided are doomed to destruction.

> Matthew 12:25 "Jesus knew their thoughts, and said to them; 'Every kingdom divided against itself is brought to desolation, and every city or house divided against itself will not stand.'"

When the degree of adversity upon a people exceeds their level of covenant unity, strife, confusion and war follow. In the face of acute food shortages, Hohokam villages most likely began to raid one another for food.[15]

Internal strife grants Satan legal access into our families, churches, businesses, cities and nations, to ravage them through various means. Therefore, out of all of the things the Lord hates, those who sow discord among brethren are at the top of His list.

Proverbs 6:16-19 "These six things the Lord hates. Yes, seven are an abomination to Him: Haughty eyes, a lying tongue, hands that shed innocent blood, a heart that devises wicked plans, feet that are swift in running to evil, a false witness who speaks lies, and one who sows discord among brethren."

Historical patterns indicate that internal strife within a people group leads to their oppression and destruction by external forces. For example, throughout the capture and enslavement of the African people during the 18th and 19th centuries, the Africans found themselves in the midst of civil war. In like manner, Scottish Celtic and Anglo-Saxon clans were at war among themselves years prior to their ongoing conflicts with the English.[16]

All Used Up

Internal strife among the Hohokam led to their oppression by the Pima Indians around 1450 A.D. According to Piman history, the Hohokam villages were led by the "Sevany", whose haughty claims of superior knowledge angered the Pima hero, Elder Brother. Elder Brother and Piman troops from the east attacked and destroyed Hohokam villages one by one along the Gila and Salt Rivers.[17]

The Pima sang the following war song during their conquest of the Hohokam:

> Look for him! Look for him!
> Poor distracted enemy; take him!
> Poor fear-stricken enemy; take him![18]

Perhaps this is why the Pimas called them the Hohokam, which means "all used up".[19]

The same elitist attitudes and haughty spirit, which led to the isolation, division and finally the destruction of the Hohokam culture, are spiritual seeds that have continued to produce similar fruit in our Valley over the years. These seeds must be repented of, rooted out and replaced with seeds of humility sown in the fear of the Lord that will bear the fruit of Christian service leading to a grand spiritual harvest of souls. Repentance, reconciliation, and reformation in the Body of Christ in the Valley of the Sun are requisite works that will spiritually prepare and position us to fulfill our corporate heavenly calling as a city of refuge, restoration, and revival.

The Hohokam provide us with a spiritual heritage that assists us in defining Greater Phoenix's divine destiny and redemptive purpose, along with unveiling some of the demonic strongholds that seek to hinder the fulfillment of our heavenly calling. Let us now venture forward into the history of the Valley of the Sun, adding more pieces along the way to our prophetic puzzle, so that together we might navigate toward our corporate destiny in God.

Chapter 3

The Rebirth of Phoenix

The origins of people, institutions, churches, cities and nations, often bring insight into their ultimate destination. To put it another way, the Alphas of life help define the purposes and means by which we reach our Omegas.

After the demise and disappearance of the Hohokam culture around the year 1450 A.D., the Salt River Valley remained virtually uninhabited for over 400 years. However, true to the Phoenician allegory, a new Phoenix began to show signs of life in 1864, when John Y. T. Smith, a former union Army officer, established a hay camp on the Hohokam site to supply forage to Camp McDowell, an army outpost 30 miles away.[1]

In the late 1860's, the new Phoenix was reborn primarily due to the labor of a visionary named John William "Jack" Swilling. Swilling was a former Confederate soldier and deserter, Union Army freighter and scout, Arizona prospector, farmer and speculator. In 1867, Swilling established the Swilling Irrigating and Canal Company in the Salt River Valley. His goal was to restore the ancient irrigation ditches of the Hohokam and recapture the Salt River Valley's rich agricultural heritage. Although Swilling suffered from alcohol and drug related problems, and later died a pauper in a Yuma jail, more than anyone else, he deserves to be called the "Father of Phoenix".[2]

The Power in a Name

Although Swilling is honored as Phoenix's founding father, an associate of Swilling's, Darrell Duppa, is credited with naming Phoenix. The Englishman Duppa was a world traveler who was lured to the Arizona frontier by the mining boom of the 1860's. He later became a stockholder in the Swilling Irrigating and Canal Company, and moved to the Salt River Valley in December 1867.[3]

Duppa named the settlement "Phoenix", after the mythical bird that rose from its own ashes, for it seemed to be an appropriate symbol of life rising anew from the remains of the past. It was predicted by Duppa and anticipated by many that the Phoenix community would be successfully built upon the ruins of the ancient Hohokam.[4] Little did Duppa realize that the Lord had used him to prophesy the divine destiny and redemptive purpose of the Salt River Valley through this simple revelation.

Throughout the Bible there are instances when the Lord named people and places after their redemptive purpose. Sometimes the Lord renamed His servants during a milestone spiritual experience wherein a divine commission was received to accomplish a specific work for God. Their old name described their current position in the kingdom of God and their new name reflected their divine destiny. Though the fulfillment of God's promises often seemed impossible, each time their new names were spoken, faith was released for the promises to be realized.

For instance, Abram, which means "exalted father", was renamed Abraham, meaning "father of a great multitude", when the Lord made an everlasting covenant with Abraham promising to make him a father of many nations (Genesis 17). The Lord also promised that Abraham's 90 year old wife Sarah, who had never been able to bear children, would bear a son named Isaac exactly one year later (Genesis 17:21).

Similarly, Jacob, which means "supplanter", was renamed Israel, meaning, "one who prevails with God" or "prince with God", after he wrestled and prevailed with the Lord Himself. Initially, Jacob secured the birthright and firstborn's blessing from his father Isaac through deception, and thus supplanted his older twin brother Esau. Nevertheless Jacob, later called Israel, was destined to lead his people as God's prince (Genesis 32:24-28).

Likewise, Simon, which means "one that hears and obeys", was one of the Lord's attentive and obedient disciples. Through the Father's revelation, Simon declared that Jesus was "the Christ, the Son of the living God". Jesus then proclaimed that Simon was Peter, meaning "rock", and that upon the rock of the Father's revelation, Jesus would build His church, and the gates of hell would not prevail against it (Matthew 16:16-18).

Finally, Saul, which means "demanded; death", initially persecuted the early church. However, after his commissioning as an apostle, his name was changed to Paul, meaning "small or little" (Acts 13:9). It was imperative that Paul stayed small in his own eyes, because the supernatural power and revelation he walked in could have easily led him into the trap of pride. Nevertheless, Paul resisted pride's temptation and developed a spirit of humility that brought exaltation to him in the kingdom of God (Matthew 18:4).

> Ephesians 3:8 "To me, who am less than the least of all the saints, this grace was given, that I should preach among the Gentiles the unsearchable riches of Christ."

Initially, Jack Swilling sought to name the new settlement in the Salt River Valley "Stonewall" after Civil War hero Stonewall Jackson.[5] The name "Stonewall", if used, would have served to further thwart the call of God upon the Valley of the Sun by assisting a spirit of rejection in building walls of isolation between its settlers. Nevertheless, the counsel of the Lord prevailed, and the name "Phoenix" was chosen over the name "Stonewall".

Just as we prophesy and solidify the destiny of our children by the words we speak over them, the divine destiny and prophetic purpose of the Valley of the Sun is affirmed every time the name "Phoenix" is spoken.

A City of Redemption

The phoenix name is thought to be of Phoenician or Greek origin. Among the Egyptians, the phoenix was sacred to the sun god, Re, and was worshipped at Heliopolis, the city of the Sun. The phoenix served as the emblem of the sun god and is associated with Osiris, the ruler of the underworld, who gave the phoenix or "Bennu" the secrets of eternal life.[6] Today, the phoenix often is used as a symbol or trade name for occult materials. For instance, a company called *Phoenix Publishing* of Custer, Washington, prints and distributes Wicca, "New Age" and occult books.[7] Based on these disturbing facts, many reading this book may ask, 'How can God use a city named after a legend with pagan and demonic origins for His divine purposes?' The answer to this question lies in Christ's redemptive nature.

The name "phoenix", although mythological and pagan in origin, can be redeemed through Christ to signify immortality, resurrection, spiritual rebirth and triumph over adversity. For instance, the phoenix was a favorite symbol on early Christian tombstones.[8] In numerous ways, the phoenix is found to be a symbol of Christ's redemptive, resurrection and restorative power.

Scripture indicates that before time began, the Lord prepared a sovereign plan and purpose for everyone's life.

II Timothy 1:9 "(Jesus) has saved us and called us with a holy calling, not according to our works, but according to His own purpose and grace, which was given to us in Christ Jesus before time began."

34

However, Satan blinds and ensnares multitudes of people and perverts their God-given talents to fulfill his demonic purposes. Those who do come to the saving knowledge of the Lord Jesus Christ frequently attempt to fulfill the plan and purpose of God in their own way, time and strength. Like Abraham, we trust in our own means and methods to produce God's promise, but give birth to an "Ishmael" instead of an "Isaac". Or like Moses, we rely on our own wisdom and strength to fulfill God's purposes, and find ourselves on a fruitless journey through a barren wilderness.

Unfortunately, our vain attempts at fulfilling our divine destiny often result in failed business endeavors, divorce, estranged children, bankruptcy or illness. In a nutshell, without Christ's redemptive intervention, countless lives paved with shattered dreams are destined for the dregs of despair leading to a quagmire of hopelessness.

Despite the disappointment and heartache that envelops millions globally, the Lord has appointed specific cities internationally to be havens of refuge and redemption for multitudes in the 21st century (Joshua 20). Phoenix, which is one of these "cities of refuge", is being transformed into an oasis of glory wherein lives and divine dreams that have been consumed by life's fires will be redeemed and resurrected to the glory of God.

A Center for Marital Restoration

In Chinese mythology, the phoenix is represented by the Feng-huang, which is a bird that symbolizes marital bliss.[9] In addition to being a city of spiritual, financial, physical and economic restoration, Phoenix is destined to be a center for marital restoration.

Currently this aspect of Greater Phoenix's redemptive purpose is being realized as Phoenix hosts an annual

International Marriage Conference which is sponsored by NAME (National Association of Marriage Enhancement). Leo Godzich, founder of NAME and a pastor at Phoenix First Assembly of God, teaches the largest Sunday school class in America, entitled "Marriage Ministry". Thousands of marriages every year are rekindled and saved from the tragedy of divorce through this ministry that is designed specifically for married couples.

Healthy, Christ-centered marriages provide a firm foundation for godly children and a strong America. Nevertheless, over the past twenty-five years, Satan has strategically utilized no-fault divorce laws to dissolve the family unit and destroy this nation. America's families have been ravaged by divorce, causing thousands of adults and children alike to suffer under the yoke of rejection and bitterness.

In 1994, Arizona was ranked 10th nationally in number of divorces per capita. In 1998, Scottsdale and Tempe were ranked 7th and 9th respectively in the nation with regard to highest divorce rate. In 1999, the divorce rate in Maricopa County was 79%.[10]

Despite the enemy's efforts to destroy the family unit, through the Covenant Marriage Movement the Lord is raising a standard in America with regard to the restoration of godly marriages, and has chosen the church in Phoenix to help spearhead this work of the Spirit. Through the prayers and efforts of Leo Godzich, NAME and many other Christians, Arizona passed a covenant marriage law on August 21, 1998. Arizona is only the second state in America to adopt a covenant marriage law, Louisiana being the first in 1997.[11]

In Arizona, couples now can choose to marry under the covenant marriage law, which requires premarital counseling and prevents couples from legal divorce except for the following circumstances: adultery, felony conviction, abandonment, physical or sexual abuse of the spouse or child, and two-year separation prior to filing for divorce. Under the covenant marriage law, married couples must seek marital counseling before any legal action can be taken to dissolve the union.[12]

Supernatural Growth

For years increasing thousands have been moving to Greater Phoenix for a new start. Saved or unsaved, married or single, employed or jobless, many are drawn by the Spirit of God to the Valley of the Sun to resurrect a dream or fulfill a destiny.

Evidence of "new life" pervading the spirits of Phoenicians can be traced back to the city's founding. In the 1950's, one new Phoenix millionaire asserted, "This country pumps new life and energy and thinking into a man!" In 1960, a Phoenix observer noted, "The mood is here; the word is out; this is the place. The city is going somewhere, and it is attracting more than an average share of people who want to go somewhere with it."[13]

Prophetically speaking, the unsaved will come in greater numbers from afar to find refuge in 21st century Phoenix, only to be spiritually reborn and redeemed to serve the purposes of God for this generation. Those servants of the Lord whose dreams have been shattered will find hope as God resurrects that which was dead and restores what Satan has stolen.

The growing need for refuge, redemption and restoration in the lives of Americans is evidenced by the fact that the Valley of the Sun is the fastest growing area in the United States today. Every year records are being broken with regard to construction, as Greater Phoenix continues to experience phenomenal growth. Of all the counties in America, Maricopa County is the fastest growing. Among the fastest growing U.S. cities with over 100,000 people, Chandler and Scottsdale are ranked second and seventh, respectively.[14] Despite man's economic explanations for this population explosion, this great ingathering of people to the Valley of the Sun is of divine origin and orchestration.

21st Century Phoenix

To prepare for this great influx of people, various ministries and Christian organizations in Phoenix and throughout the United States have planned major evangelistic and prayer outreaches in the Valley of the Sun. For example, Mission America's *Celebrate Jesus 2000* campaign, whose vision was to pray for and present the gospel to every man, woman and young person in the nation by the year 2000, chose Phoenix as their primary pilot target. Greater Phoenix was chosen because it is the fastest growing city in the United States and has city-wide networks of pastors, youth workers and prayer leaders. In concert with this initiative, the North American Mission Board of the Southern Baptist Convention sowed into this valley-wide movement by investing 2.5 million dollars and some three to four thousand volunteers into Phoenix through the year 2000.[15]

The unity of the Spirit among churches in the Valley of the Sun is of utmost importance for Greater Phoenix to fulfill its destiny as a city of refuge in the 21st century. Therefore, thousands of Christians from several churches and ministries in the valley assembled at Bank One Ballpark on January 15, 2000, to make a prophetic declaration of unity and Christ's Lordship over the Valley of the Sun. This event, entitled, *Festival of Faith 2000*, was "a gathering of the Body of Christ to commemorate the birth of Christ, to celebrate our faith in Christ, and to commit ourselves to the mission of Christ in the new millennium."[16]

When revival waters flood a city, a greater percentage of the population will seek higher ground, that they might plant their lives solidly on the Rock, Jesus Christ. To accommodate this great influx of seekers, some churches in the Valley of the Sun are planning ahead. For example, Phoenix First Assembly of God, which ministers to thousands every Sunday, adopted a three year plan called *Vision 2000* to raise the funds necessary to build more buildings to accommodate the swelling crowds that will be seeking Christ in the revival that is soon to come. In anticipation of this spiritual awakening, Phoenix First Assembly of God has also planted a new church in Scottsdale, AZ.

It is my prayer that every pastor and Christian leader in the Valley of the Sun sense the urgency of the hour and make preparations in the natural and spiritual realms, that they might participate in this grand harvest of souls.

Chapter 4

Arising From The Ashes

A surface examination of a city's origins can provide a fundamental understanding of its redemptive purpose and divine destiny. However, an in-depth, prayerful study of a city's development is crucial to discovering God's prophetic plan for fulfilling that redemptive purpose through His people.

Building the Old Waste Places

While passing through the Salt River Valley in November of 1867, Jack Swilling noticed the ruins of the Hohokam irrigation system and pondered the agricultural potential of the area. In December, after garnering finances from supporters in nearby Wickenburg and hiring sixteen workers, Swilling moved his newly organized Swilling Irrigating and Canal Company to the Salt River Valley to commence soil cultivation.[1]

Swilling and company secured land north of the Salt River and cleaned out old irrigation ditches originally built by the Hohokam and constructed new ones.[2] This work of restoration, upon which Phoenix was founded, is key in understanding the Valley of the Sun's redemptive purpose.

> Isaiah 61:4 "And they shall rebuild the old ruins. They shall raise up the former desolations, and they shall repair the ruined cities, the desolations of many desolations."

Despite the fact that neither Swilling nor any of the other major founders of Phoenix were spiritual men, pro-

40

phetic destiny can be extracted from the original purposes for which Phoenix was established. Swilling's restoration of the ancient water-carrying channels set the stage for the restoration and habitation of the Salt River Valley. Hohokam canals continued to be restored by irrigators, and thousands of additional acres of fertile land were brought into cultivation. By 1878, three major canals, the Salt River Valley Canal, the Maricopa Canal and the Grand Canal, irrigated a large portion of the valley which produced a tremendous yield and variety of crops. Phoenix quickly became known as the "Garden City of Arizona".[3]

Ezekiel 36:34,35   "Thus says the Lord God: The desolate land shall be tilled instead of lying desolate in the sight of all who pass by. So they will say, **'This land that was desolate has become like the garden of Eden**; and the wasted, desolate, and ruined cities are now fortified and inhabited.'"

The Arizona Canal

In December of 1882, local promoters and land developer, Clark A. Churchill, incorporated the Arizona Canal Company. Their mission was to build the widest (36 ft.) and longest (41 mi.) canal in the Salt River Valley, that would open eighty thousand acres to cultivation. This canal would be unique in that it would not be built upon the ancient Hohokam canal system or extensions of it.[4]

In May of 1883, William J. Murphy, a former Union Army officer and veteran of the Civil War from Illinois, under contract by the Arizona Canal Company, commenced work on the Arizona Canal. Payment for the contract was to be entirely in stocks and bonds of the Arizona Canal Company. This necessitated the sale of bonds to obtain money for operating expenses. He sold some of these bonds in Chicago, New York, San Francisco, Boston and even overseas in London and Edinburgh.[5]

The strict contract that Murphy accepted required that the canal be completed to a certain point by February 15, 1884, else he would forfeit the contract and all unpaid balances for work already completed. Just prior to the 15th of February, an attempt by conspirators was made to cause Murphy to fail to complete the canal to the specified point, while he was in San Francisco raising money to pay off his subcontractor. During that time, telegraph lines were down, cutting Phoenix off from any outside communication.[6]

Despite the conspirators efforts to induce the subcontractors to quit work, one loyal subcontractor continued working and completed the specified portion of the canal at 10 AM on the day that the contract required that it should be completed by noon. During this emergency, William Christy, Murphy's friend, fellow developer and Iowa banker, came to his aid and shortly thereafter in April 1884 organized the Valley Bank of Phoenix. In June 1885, the Arizona Canal was completed.[7]

In October of 1886, Murphy, as grading contractor, also helped build the Maricopa and Phoenix railroad, which linked Phoenix to the outside world. In July of 1887 the railroad was completed. Like the Arizona Canal, the Maricopa and Phoenix Railroad proved to be a valuable asset in the development of the city and the Salt River Valley.[8]

In June of 1887, Murphy, Christy and Churchill formed the Arizona Improvement Company, a water and land development company that conducted an aggressive promotion campaign which persuaded many new farmers to settle on the land irrigated by the Arizona Canal. In 1888, they also planned and built Grand Avenue, which linked downtown Phoenix to the newly irrigated land.

Along Grand Avenue, the company surveyed and promoted the townsites of Alhambra, Peoria and Glendale.[9]

W.J. Murphy, being a great lover of trees, planted 33 miles of trees along the avenues of Phoenix. He also planted 635 acres of orange and grapefruit trees, 700 acres of apricots, peaches, almonds and grapes which were shipped from Glendale to eastern markets. In 1901, Murphy met and found favor with President Roosevelt, who issued a government order that protected the watershed of the Salt and Verde Rivers, which was vital to maintaining the water supply to the Salt River Valley.[10]

Rivers in the Desert

The preceding historical account of William J. Murphy, which summarizes his great contributions to the development of Phoenix and the Salt River Valley, is pregnant with latent prophetic parallels that help define the purpose and divine destiny of the Valley of the Sun.

Notice first, that within the name of Clark A. Churchill, the leader of the Arizona Canal Corporation, is the word "Church". The Arizona Canal Corporation, which conceived and inspired the building of the Arizona Canal, is likened unto the Church of Jesus Christ, through which the Lord's purposes are birthed, developed and fulfilled.

The Arizona Canal was unique. It was not built upon the old Hohokam canal system, but upon soil that had been previously unplowed. Due to its great size, the Arizona Canal significantly impacted the development of Phoenix. Similarly, the work that the Lord has planned to do through the Church in the Valley of the Sun will be new and different, not conforming to common historical trends of spiritual renewal. A spiritual work of repentance, reconciliation and revival wrought within the valley-wide Church will transform Greater Phoenix into a spiritual refuge for the void spirits and hopeless souls of thousands who will be migrating to our valley in need of spiritual regeneration and restoration.

> Isaiah 43:18,19 "Do not remember the former things, nor consider the things of old. Behold, I will do a new thing, now it shall spring forth; shall you not know it?"

W. J. Murphy, referred to as "the dreamer", prophetically represents those pioneers of the faith whom the Lord has sent and will send to the Valley of the Sun to spearhead this unique work of God. Like Murphy, these selfless men and women have a vision and dream from God for which they will sacrifice everything to witness its fulfillment. Murphy was relentless in his efforts to complete the Arizona Canal, which supplied life-giving water to the land and people of the Valley of the Sun. In like manner, these spiritual pioneers will be zealous in their prayer effort to the end that the Church of Greater Phoenix may experience a baptism of repentance resulting in a flood of reconciliation and spiritual revival throughout our valley. Even the unsaved and callous of heart will acknowledge and honor the coming visitation of God.

> Isaiah 43:20 "The beast of the field will honor Me, the jackals and the ostriches, because I give waters in the wilderness and rivers in the desert, to give drink to My people, My chosen."

In any significant work of God, opposition and persecution will come from among the ranks. At a critical moment, W. J. Murphy was betrayed by the majority of those who worked for him in building the Arizona Canal. He would have lost everything if it weren't for one faithful subcontractor and a man by the name of William Christy,

44

who came to his aid in time of need. In like manner, the emerging spiritual pioneers of Phoenix will experience rejection and persecution by much of the Church. Nevertheless, there will remain a faithful remnant who will be true to the pioneers of God and see the work completed.

Notice that the name of William Christy, one of the men to stand by Murphy in times of crisis, contains the word "Christ". Christ, translated Messiah in Hebrew, means "anointed one". Like Shadrach, Meshach and Abed-Nego of the Old Testament, who were delivered from the fire by the Son of God, these spiritual pioneers will be preserved and delivered from fiery opposition by the living Christ, and will witness the fulfillment of their divine dream (Daniel 3:25).

A Road In the Wilderness

Murphy not only completed the Arizona Canal, but also contributed to the building of the Maricopa and Phoenix Railroad which linked the Salt River Valley to the outside world. Similarly, the unique work of restoration that will take place in Phoenix will be exported through these spiritual pioneers to other cities throughout the world.

Murphy, Christy and Churchill also built Grand Avenue, which extended through the land irrigated by the Arizona Canal. Grand Avenue is representative of the wide path that will be constructed in the spirit realm on which thousands will be washed by the baptism of repentance and drink from the well of salvation.

Isaiah 43:19 "I will even make a road in the wilderness and rivers in the desert."

The miles of fruit trees that Murphy planted are indicative of the multitude of believers that will bring forth much fruit. The fruit consists of souls saved, lives changed, and dreams restored and fulfilled. The fruit produced by Murphy's trees and fields were shipped across the United States from a newly established colony called Glendale.

The Temperance Colony of Glendale

The founding of Glendale can be directly attributed to the construction of the Arizona Canal, the opening of irrigatable lands in the valley and the promotional efforts of Murphy. In 1891, Murphy convinced B.A. Hadsell of Chicago, a well known and successful colonizer of temperance communities, to begin an intensive campaign to attract members of the Church of the Brethren from Glendale, Pennsylvania to settle the "Temperance Colony of Glendale". From 1892 through 1895, Hadsell succeeded in soliciting about seventy families of colonizers to the Glendale area.[11]

The following is a portion of an 1892 Arizona Weekly Gazette advertisement that was used to attract prospective colonists.[12]

ATTENTION IS CALLED TO THE
Temperance Colony of Glendale
THE SALE OF INTOXICANTS
IS FOREVER FORBIDDEN
IN THE CONVEYANCE OF THE LAND

School Houses and Churches,
But no saloons or gambling houses! No drunken brawls!
No jails! and no paupers!

An 1894 article in the Phoenix Herald contained a similar promotion of the "Temperance Colony of Glendale".[13]

46

"Believing that saloons and intemperance are a curse to good society, Mr. Hadsell founded this colony on the temperance plan, having the land on which Glendale is situated, and from one to two miles around it is deeded with restrictions that in case a saloon be established the owner forfeits all right and the property reverts back to the original owner. Good temperate people greatly desire to locate their families in such a colony, away from shame and evil associations, and where church and school privileges can be had."

W.J. Murphy's sense of the divine calling on and unique purpose for the Valley of the Sun inspired him to work with every fiber of his being to develop Greater Phoenix. Although his purpose was to plant seeds of destiny, as with most visionaries, he was driven to witness the fruit of his labors. As a result, he set out to establish this utopia in Glendale comprised of temperate saints from other lands.

Despite B.A. Hadsell's apparent success in "selling" these churched immigrants on relocating to the "Temperance Colony of Glendale", violations of gambling and of the temperance clause were reported shortly after the colony's establishment. The flood of 1897 and the three years of drought that followed forced many of the temperate immigrants to "sell out" and move to California at the turn of the century. The temperance regulations that early officials tried to enforce were overruled by the county and state governments.[14]   Although B.A. Hadsell's intentions in promoting the "Temperance Colony of Glendale" were good, it turned out to be a "bad sell". Notice that B.A. Hadsell's name is prophetically encrypted "BAHad sell", which is translated "Bad Sell".

Interestingly enough, Winfield Scott, the founder of Scottsdale, was an Army chaplain and Baptist revivalist preacher who also sought to establish his settlement in

Christian righteousness and purity. He attempted to accomplish this end by forming the first Anti-Saloon League in the Arizona Territory in 1897. One Phoenix reporter commented that Scott preached temperance and "it is the determination of the first settler of Scottsdale never to let alcohol get a foothold in this part of the valley."[15]

Temperance colonies, where abstinence from the worldly pleasures of gambling, liquor and prostitution are imposed upon their settlers, have had little success in enforcing their imposed standards and even less impact in affecting people with the Gospel of Jesus Christ. In fact, the idea of building a spiritual utopia, where there are only "school houses and churches, but no saloons, gambling houses, drunken brawls, jails or paupers", is not only idealistic but unscriptural.

Jesus never commanded His Church to build spiritual communes but to go and make disciples in all nations (Matthew 28:19). The early Church's commune in the Book of Acts didn't last very long either, as Jesus allowed persecution to disperse the Church to the uttermost parts of the earth (Acts 2:44-47; 5:1-10; 8:1).

A Valley in the Valley

Glen literally means "a secluded narrow valley", and the word "dale" simply means "valley". Glendale can then be translated "a secluded narrow valley in a valley". A more applicable interpretation of the word Glendale as it applies to the Phoenix area is "a valley in the Valley of the Sun". In Scripture, valleys represent death or times of trial and heartache.

Psalm 23:4 "Yea, though I walk through the valley of the shadow of death, I will fear no evil, for You are with me."

Prophetically speaking, the Valley of the Sun will continue to draw the brokenhearted, the hopeless, and downtrodden. From their valley of hopelessness and despair, the Lord will draw these lost souls to drink and eat from the tree and river of everlasting life. Some will remain in the Valley of the Sun, but others will return from where they came to testify of Christ's redemptive and restorative power. They will no longer be without hope, but be empowered by the dream seeds that were placed within them as newborn sons and daughters of God.

A Foundation of Many Generations

Soon after the completion of the Arizona Canal, lumber companies in the northern part of the state cut much of the timber off the water sheds of the Verde and Salt Rivers, thus threatening the water supply to the Salt River Valley. However in 1901, Murphy's plea to President Roosevelt to maintain a forest reserve around the watershed of the Salt and Verde Rivers was heard and the water supply was protected.[16]

In a similar manner, the enemy will ferociously attack believers in the Valley, seeking to cut off the flow of revival waters and thus threaten the continual harvest of souls. On the average, true revival lasts about 36 months.[17] Revival wanes when the saints fail to continue seeking the Lord and preserve hard won spiritual victories. However, Greater Phoenician spiritual pioneers will plead to God our Father in behalf of the saints in the valley, and they will be delivered from the oppression and distractions of the enemy. As a result, the revival harvest in the Valley of the Sun will continue well into the 21st century.

The work of William J. Murphy transcended his life span, touching the hearts of and establishing a prophetic pattern for other "dreamers" who have come and will come to the Valley of the Sun to impact multitudes for the glory and kingdom of God.

> Isaiah 58:12 "Those from among you shall build the old waste places. You shall raise up the foundations of many generations; and you shall be called the Repairer of the Breach, The Restorer of Streets to Dwell In."

The following excerpt from William J. Murphy's obituary testifies of his great vision that became a foundation for many generations of dreamers that would follow.

> "Mr. Murphy saw the realization of only a part of his vision, but he so developed that vision that it will perhaps within the span of the years of the present generation grow into a complete reality.
> Mr. Murphy worked because he loved to work, not for selfish ends but for the people then in the valley and the people to come in.
> He saw not with the eyes of an individual but with the eyes of his generation and the generation unborn.
> He saw the completed canal in vision. That to him was the great fact. The details, dismal as they were, could not, and did not, dim the vision, and the work proceeded under many handicaps until it was finished and the lands and people blessed with water."[18]

The themes of refuge, restoration, and revival will continually rise to the surface as we investigate Christ's redemptive purpose for Greater Phoenix. Truly it is a privilege to have been positioned by God in the Valley of the Sun for such a time as this. Let us all take seriously this once-in-a-lifetime opportunity, that we might all fulfill the purposes of God for our generation.

Chapter 5

Defining Phoenix's Divine Destiny

Despite the myriad of people and events that comprise the 100-plus year modern history of Phoenix, relatively few of them significantly contribute to the comprehension of the prophetic purpose and plan of God for the Valley of the Sun. In fact, some of the key people and events are long forgotten, carefully hidden in Phoenix's historical fabric, only to be prophetically uncovered and examined one thread at a time.

A Haven For Health Seekers

Phoenix promoters used the drawing power of the climate to attract health seekers to the desert oasis. Those "chasing the cure" were told that Phoenix was "the healthiest city in the known world". Physicians in the eastern U.S. proclaimed time and again that "the one cure for lung trouble is desert air". These types of advertisements and testimonials resulted in an influx of patients with various respiratory problems from all over the country, transforming Phoenix and the Valley of the Sun into a "lungers' Mecca" by the turn of the 20th century.[1]

St. Joseph's Hospital, St. Luke's Home, and the Desert Inn Sanatorium provided the best care and accommodations for the affluent health seekers. However, indigent health seekers were forced outside the city to reside in tents in poor desert settlements such as Sunnyslope, where they endured a life of rejection, isolation and destitution.[2]

However, Christianna Gilchrist, a school teacher from Colorado, moved to Phoenix in 1899 for health reasons and led an endeavor which provided care for indigent health seekers in the Valley of the Sun. In addition to her active work in the Women's Christian Temperance Union and the Presbyterian Missionary Society, she spent many years as supervisor of the Associated Charities in Phoenix, which provided much aid to poor health seekers.[3]

Despite helping over 300 people during the winter of 1907-1908, Gilchrist lamented the "great draft on charity in Phoenix". Nevertheless, she worked diligently over the years to overcome this problem and through her example eventually inspired many Phoenicians to devote time and money to the problems of poor health seekers and others in need of assistance. One reporter of the Gazette observed, "The people have come to know her as a patient, faithful worker of the Lord and give without stint".[4]

Christianna Gilchrist's name contains the word "Christ" not only in her first name, but also in her last name. Prophetically, her life and ministry are uniquely representative of Christ's redemptive purpose and calling upon Greater Phoenix, and deserve closer examination.

A 21st Century City of Refuge

In the Old Testament, after Joshua and the children of Israel conquered the Canaanites and drove them from their "promised land", the Lord commanded Joshua to establish six cities of refuge.

> Joshua 20:1,2   The Lord also spoke to Joshua saying, "Speak to the children of Israel, saying, 'Appoint for yourselves **cities of refuge**, of which I spoke to you through Moses.'"

Similarly, today the Lord is establishing cities of refuge throughout the world, where people can find refuge from life's hardships, recover from heartache and disappointment, dream again and begin again. Christianna Gilchrist's ministry to the ailing health of the poor foreshadows Christ's redemptive, restorative calling upon the Church in the Valley of the Sun to establish Greater Phoenix as a city of refuge for millions in the 21st century.

Phoenix has already established itself as a place of refuge for the retired rich, who annually escape the harsh winters of the North to be refreshed by the Valley of the Sun's pleasant climate. These "snowbirds" glide into the Valley of the Sun at Winter's dawn and fly out in the Spring, rested, rejuvenated and full of life.

But what of the poor, the undereducated, the foreigner, the solitary, the diseased and the sinner, whose wings have also been damaged by the storms of life? Through the 1980s, Phoenix continued as the national leader in divorce, suicide, substance abuse, and mental illness.[5] Every year since 1995, approximately 2300 refugees from countries around the world come to Arizona seeking refuge from the political turmoil of their native countries. As a result, one local pastor commented, "It's a big melting pot here. It's like living in a miniature United Nations."[6] Are the poor, the sick and the refugee to continue to come to this valley of dreams only to be rejected, isolated and left to die in a nest of dejection and destitution? If we fear the Lord and sincerely endeavor to fulfill our unique Christian corporate commission, the answer to these questions must be an emphatic "No!". Like Christianna Gilchrist, we must champion the cause of those less unfortunate, who like anyone else, deserve a second chance at succeeding in life.

Malachi 4:2 "But to you who fear My name, the Sun of Righteousness shall arise with healing in His wings."

Phoenician history provides us with yet another prophetic analogy that solidifies the Valley of the Sun's divine call to this unique ministry of restoration. Luke Air Force Base, located here in the valley, was named after

Frank Luke, Jr., who was a famous Phoenix born flying ace during World War I.[7] Interestingly enough, "Luke" also is the name of the gospel writer who was a physician by profession. One Bible commentator noted, "Luke's gospel reveals his concern for the poor, sick, and outcast, thus offering a clue to why Paul called him 'the beloved physician' (Col. 4:14)".[8] Prophetically speaking, the Valley of the Sun is destined to be a hospital for the broken and hurting, a place where damaged wings are restored and new flight plans made, thus enabling many to soar to greater heights and reach their divine destination to the glory of God.

The Salt River Project

Organized in 1903, the Salt River Project (SRP), which was named after the Salt River that flows through the Valley of the Sun, is a natural representation of a supernatural work that the Lord desires to do in and through His Church here. The Salt River Project over the years has developed and maintained the 131 miles of canals that supply domestic and irrigation water to the Valley of the Sun.[9] Water, whether in the form of fountains, rivers or streams, is indicative of life, as was discussed in detail in Chapter 1. Salt, on the other hand, represents the grace and peace needed to produce covenant unity in the Body of Christ.

Mark 9:50   "Have salt in yourselves, and have peace with one another."

Colossians 4:6   "Let your speech always be with grace, seasoned with salt, that you may know how you ought to answer each one."

Salt also signifies the flavor of Christ that believers exude to the lost world around them. Our salty savor of the Savior causes unsaved mankind to thirst for the living waters of salvation found in Christ.

Matthew 5:13   "You are the salt of the earth; but if the salt loses its flavor, how shall it be seasoned?"

Since the future of the Valley of the Sun is dependent on the availability and abundance of water, the success of the Salt River Project is crucial to the stability, prosperity, and growth of Greater Phoenix. In the same way, the success of the Lord's Salt River Project will determine the intensity and longevity of the revival fires that are destined to engulf the Valley of the Sun in the 21st century.

God's Enrichment vs. Man's Promotion

Despite the Lord's plans for prospering the Valley of the Sun, since the founding of Phoenix, ambitious men have sought to promote the area through a technique commonly referred to as "boosterism". Advertisements and testimonials concerning the valley's temperate and health restoring climate, year-round growing season, and economic and industrial opportunities have drawn thousands to the Valley of the Sun for over 100 years. In the early 1900s, the most popular promotional slogan, "The Five C's", included copper, cattle, cotton, citrus and climate, yet excluded the most important "C", namely Christ.[10]

Though Arizona's state motto is, "Ditat Deus", which means "God Enriches", the Valley of the Sun's growth and success to date appear to be largely due to the pursuits and efforts of ambitious men.[11]

Psalm 65:9,10 "You give attention to the earth and water it. **You greatly enrich it.** The river of God is full of water. You provide their grain, for so You have prepared it. You water its ridges abundantly. You settle its furrows. You make it soft with showers. You bless its growth."

Selfish ambition even characterized Phoenix's founder Jack Swilling, who contracted "gold fever" in 1867 and pursued his would be fortune at the Vulture Gold Mine in Vulture City, near modern-day Wickenburg, Arizona. Interestingly enough, Michael Goldwater, the grandfather of Barry Goldwater, who represented Arizona in the U.S. Senate until 1987, helped finance the Vulture Gold Mine and stamp mill.[12]

Probably more than any other single family, the Goldwaters have significantly impacted the course of Phoenix and the entire state of Arizona. The Goldwater name contains a prophetic meaning that characterizes the means of Arizona's establishment since its inception. In our context, "Gold" symbolizes the vainglorious pursuits of men and the strength expended by men to attain them. Once again, "water" signifies life. In a nutshell, the Goldwater name, with all due respect, prophetically represents the self-serving efforts of men in accomplishing viable and valuable ends without the acknowledgment or assistance of God.

The passing of Barry Goldwater in May of 1998 prophetically marks the end of an era, and the dawning of a new era, wherein the purposes of God for Phoenix and Arizona will be accomplished by God-fearing, Spirit-led men and women.

Ezekiel 36:36 "Then the nations which are left all around you shall know that I, the Lord, have rebuilt the ruined places and planted what was desolate. I, the Lord, have spoken it, and will do it."

These ambassadors of Christ will serve as tools in the hand of the Master Builder, and humbly acknowledge that it is Christ working in and through them to rebuild this once desolate valley of ruins into a valley full of God's glory.

Winning the War Over the Prince of the Air

This rebuilding process will not be accomplished without a fight, for indeed the devil has historically set out to keep the Lily of the Valley out of the Valley of the Sun. From the Hohokam wars with the Pimas, to the Mexican War of 1848, wherein the United States acquired the land now known as New Mexico and Arizona, to the white man's numerous conflicts with the Apache Indians, war has characterized the Valley of the Sun.

The commencement of World War II triggered an economic boom and population explosion in Phoenix. The war years saw the activation of several military installations in the valley, and were followed by the establishment of defense industries. Since the Valley of the Sun offered level surfaces, clear skies, little rainfall and the "rarity of high winds", it became a most appealing site to develop "a huge air program in the sun" during World War II. As a result, thousands of American and foreign cadets trained at the Valley of the Sun's numerous air fields, including Luke Field, Williams Field, Thunderbird II, and Litchfield Naval Air Facility. In fact, by the end of the war, Luke Field became the world's largest advanced flight training school, as more than 13,500 pilots had received their wings.[13]

Even as Phoenix has served as a training ground in the natural for air battle, the army of God in the Valley of the Sun must be trained to spiritually combat the host of wickedness in heavenly places that threatens our spiritual atmosphere (Ephesians 2:2). For indeed, the prince of the power of the air must first be cast down so that the Sun of

Righteousness can arise with healing in His wings to redeem, revive and restore the multitudes that are being drawn into this valley of dreams (Malachi 4:2).

> II Corinthians 10:4   "For the weapons of our warfare are not of the flesh but mighty in God for pulling down strongholds."

However, prior to the Church engaging in spiritual warfare with these enemies of the Lord's glory, they must first be clearly identified. The following section of this book will help us uncover these demonic strongholds, discover their weaknesses, and provide a measure of wisdom on how to secure their defeat (Ecclesiastes 9:18).

Section II

Defeating Demonic Deterrents to Greater Phoenix's Divine Destiny

Chapter 6

The Valley's Wise Master Builder

Scripture testifies that Satan's primary mission is to kill, steal from and destroy mankind (John 10:10). However, to better understand how Satan devours and destroys, we must first understand how God blesses and builds. Every marriage, home, business, organization, church or city conceived in the heart of the Father is built by the Lord in three principal ways: By revelation, through relationships, and over generations. In a nutshell, God builds on purpose, with people, for posterity.

Building On Purpose

The chief cornerstone in the foundation of every divinely inspired endeavor is "The Rock", Jesus Christ (Ephesians 2:19,20). No matter how successful our pursuits appear to be, without Christ as our foundation, our labor is at best vain and the eternal value of our accomplishments is worthless (I Corinthians 3:11-15). Therefore, our surrender to and salvation through the Lord Jesus Christ is the foundation upon which the Lord can build in us His divine dreams and prophetic purposes.

Once the foundation of Christ is established in our lives, the Lord then begins building purpose in us through revelation. Jesus declared to His disciples that He would build His Church on the rock of divine revelation, and the gates of hell would not prevail against it (Matthew 16:18). Revelation concerning our divine purpose can be communicated through dreams, visions, prophecy or simply through an idea.

Where there is no vision, people perish (Proverbs 29:18). A well-known minister once expressed this truth by saying, "A man can live thirty days without food, three days without water, but only three minutes without purpose." Unfortunately, many today are disillusioned, discouraged and bitterly brooding over dreams that have been shattered through betrayal, disappointment and injustice.

> Proverbs 13:12   "Hope deferred make the heart sick, but when the desire comes, it is a tree of life."

Despite the heartache that millions experience due to broken dreams, the Lord is raising up cities of refuge and ministers of reconciliation to embrace and heal the brokenhearted, that they might again thrive under the revelation and inspiration of a divine dream.

In the first section of this book, we discovered that the Lord not only has a purpose for individual lives, but also a specific corporate calling upon individual cities. In the Valley of the Sun, our destiny to become a 21st century city of restoration and refuge can only be realized after we first have corporately conceived in the womb of our spirit this revelatory seed concerning Greater Phoenix's divine purpose. In the following chapter, we will uncover Satan's scheme to deceive thousands of Phoenicians by attempting to pervert our prophetic purpose so that we might pursue a counterfeit calling.

Building With People

The second way that God builds is with people. Interactive, interdependent relationships are vital to the success of any dream, especially a corporate dream. The Lord designed His kingdom in such a way that our individual purpose in life cannot be fully realized without our participation in the fulfillment of the dreams of others. That is why God cannot build with loners or recluses, because their lives begin and end with self.

History has proven that groups of people, who have put their minds, hearts and resources together to accomplish a certain task, no matter how difficult, are usually successful. For example, in the book of Genesis, when the inhabitants of the earth corporately decided to build a tower to reach the heavens and make a name for themselves, God Himself acknowledged that they could do it unless they were somehow divided. Therefore, He confused their language (Genesis 11:1-9).

> Genesis 11:6 "And the Lord said, 'Indeed the people are one and they all have one language, and this is what they begin to do; now nothing that they propose to do will be withheld from them'."

If heathens can succeed by exercising the principles of unity, how much more should we then, as children of God, endeavor to keep the unity of the Spirit in the bond of peace that we might fulfill the purposes of God for our generation (Ephesians 4:3).

Paul, having a revelation concerning the utmost importance of maintaining the unity of the Spirit, begged the Corinthian church to walk together as one. I also make this same plea concerning the unity of the Spirit to the Body of Christ in the Valley of the Sun.

> I Corinthians 1:10 "Now I plead with you, brethren, by the name of our Lord Jesus Christ, that you all speak the same thing, and that there be no divisions among you, but that you be perfectly joined together in the same mind and in the same judgment."

Despite Satan's master plan to divide and conquer the people of God in the Valley of the Sun, if we will endeavor to pursue the unity of the Spirit, we will be victorious and witness the glory of God.

Building For Posterity

The third way that God builds is for posterity or future generations. All too often we build businesses, churches and ministries without considering or making provision for those who will come after us.

In the Old Testament, Jehovah was referred to by Israel as the God of Abraham, Isaac and Jacob. Because of Abraham's covenant with the Lord, Israel enjoyed a profound, patriarchal spiritual heritage and blessing that was passed down from generation to generation.

> Psalm 105:8,9 "He has remembered His covenant forever, the word which He commanded, for a thousand generations, the covenant which He made with Abraham."

Similarly, the Lord, Who is the wise Master Builder, desires to impart greater anointing and superior wisdom to each succeeding generation of the Church. Only then will we, through Christ, successfully impact the world with the soul-saving message and life-changing ministry of Jesus Christ.

As we come to the end of the age, it is imperative that we build with God's end in mind and not our own.

> Psalm 112:1,2 "Blessed is the man who fears the Lord, who delights greatly in His commandments. His descendants will be mighty on earth; the generation of the upright will be blessed."

In the fear of the Lord, we must only build what the Lord has commanded, so that future generations of the Church will be upright, blessed and mighty in the earth.

Provision For the Vision

Sometimes it is difficult to discern whether a particular work is a "God idea" or merely a "good idea". Nevertheless, there are three Biblical standards or principles by which we can determine if a work is born of and built by God. The first principle is, *"When God guides, He provides."* Provision of financial and personnel resources for any work He has ordained will always be sufficient. Too often we expect God to promote and fund projects that He didn't originate (Proverbs 3:5,6).

> Psalm 127:1 "Unless the Lord builds the house, they labor in vain who build it. Unless the Lord guards the city, the watchman stays awake in vain."

This second principle is, *"What God directs, he protects."* The Lord will guard every work that He has ordained. Many times we pursue an idea that looks good or worked for someone else without inquiring of the Lord. As a result, when our church, ministry or business is devoured by the enemy, we blame God.

The third principle is, *"What God induces always produces."* Every work ordained of God will bear fruit during its harvest season. In other words, the endeavor will grow, endure and positively impact lives for Jesus Christ (John 15:1-8).

Dream Savers or Dream Slayers?

With a greater understanding concerning God's building process, we can more easily understand how Satan devours and destroys. We have learned that the Lord builds through revelation of purpose through a unified people. On the contrary, Satan destroys primarily through deception and division. Nevertheless, the Lord has given His

65

children authority over Satan and his hordes, along with the wisdom and power to execute their defeat (II Corinthians 2:11, Psalm 149:6-9).

> Luke 10:19   "Behold, I give you the authority to **trample on serpents and scorpions**, and over all the power of the enemy, and nothing shall by any means hurt you."

All divine dreams originate in the heart and mind of God. Truly, He is the "Dream Maker". However, every day people speak words and perform works that either positively or negatively effect the dream seeds that the Lord has placed in the hearts of every human being. We either help "save" the dreams or "slay" the dreams of others.

Knowing that the Lord's redemptive purpose for the Valley of the Sun entails providing refuge and refreshing for weary bodies and wounded souls, redemption to lost spirits, and restored hope to the broken dreams of thousands, let us forge ahead to uncover the deceptive and dividing devices that Satan has utilized specifically throughout Greater Phoenix to plunder God's purposes.

Chapter 7

Deceived By Divination

Deception is Satan's first line of defense in keeping people from reaching their divine destiny. If the "father of lies" can distract us from realizing God's purpose for our individual lives, he can ensure that we never fulfill our high calling. Knowing that the Lord builds our lives on revelation concerning His purposes, Satan attempts to destroy mankind by perverting spiritual truths and propagating lies (II Corinthians 11:4).

> Hosea 4:6 "My people are destroyed for a lack of knowledge."

The Father's primary purpose for all humanity is "that none should perish, but that all should come to repentance" (II Peter 3:9). On the contrary, Satan's primary goal is to keep Christ, the Chief Cornerstone, out of the foundation of as many lives as possible (Ephesians 2:20). He then can ensure that our temples are either completely destroyed or built void of Christ and the glory of the Father.

Antichrists and False Christs

Deception and denial concerning the deity and saving power of Jesus Christ is the platform from which the spirit of antichrist launches its attacks (I John 4:3). For example, the antichrist spirit that has infiltrated the United States, promotes good will and works, morality, equality and even religion, yet vehemently opposes the name, gospel and power of Jesus Christ.

I John 2:22   "Who is a liar but he who denies that Jesus is the Christ? He is antichrist who denies the Father and the Son."

The goal of the antichrist spirit is to deceive people into believing in and following a counterfeit christ or "false christ".

Matthew 24:24   "For false christs and false prophets will arise and show great signs and wonders, so as to deceive, if possible, even the elect."

False christs promise truth, liberty, prosperity, and peace to their disciples, yet ultimately enslave and drown them in a quagmire of deception, despair, and spiritual death. False christs are usually spiritual in nature, yet sometimes manifest as idols which take the rightful place of Jesus Christ in the hearts of mankind (I John 5:20,21). Fueled by the antichrist spirit, some of the most popular American idols or false christs that are promising salvation to millions today are the internet, the stock market, gambling, food, technology, sex, drugs, music, alcohol, diet and exercise, careers, computers, television, movies and sports.

Sedona and the New Age Movement

When false christs leave people empty and searching for more, Satan offers other deceptions, usually a form of divination, to satisfy thirsty souls in search of spiritual fulfillment and contentment. The latest, most popular form of divination that has beguiled millions over the past several years has been termed "New Age".

The New Age Movement is fueled by a spirit of divination and is designed by Satan to captivate the masses through the intriguing and bizarre operation of familiar spirits. Familiar spirits are demonic counterparts of guard-

68

ian angels that surround and acquaint themselves with people. Mediums and psychics, through a spirit of divination, communicate with familiar spirits that often reveal specific information about people. Although those who operate under a spirit of divination may accurately reveal one's hidden past, present or future, the source of their inspiration ultimately brings deception, defilement and destruction.

Divination is a form of witchcraft that operates under counterfeit spiritual authority and is the opposite of the true gift of prophecy, which is administered under the unction of the Holy Spirit. Some common old world names for those who operate under a spirit of divination include witches, sorcerers, diviners, soothsayers, fortunetellers, palm readers, tarot card readers, false prophets, etc. In this "New Age Movement", the same old spirit of divination enables mediums and psychics to captivate and manipulate thousands to follow the counsel of familiar spirits.

Sedona, Arizona, which is considered by many to be the New Age capital of the United States, has surfaced in recent years to supply America's growing demand for supernatural encounters. As a result, Sedona and the nearby Red Rock Secret Mountain Wilderness have become one of the most accommodating sites in the world for contemporary spiritual pilgrims in search of metaphysical experiences.[1] Recently, an archivist of special collections at Northern Arizona University in Flagstaff reported that a church to worship aliens recently was established in Sedona.[2] These so called aliens that are being worshipped are nothing more than demons.

Unfortunately, this New Age Mecca, with its purported energy vortexes and psychic phenomenon, has served to distract and detour thousands not only from realizing their prophetic purpose, but more importantly, from receiving Jesus Christ.

This form of divination has infiltrated Greater Phoenix over the past several years, has contaminated the minds and hearts of many, and has become as a spiritual stronghold in the Valley of the Sun.

Misled By Mormonism

Another powerful source of deception that Satan has used to bewitch multitudes in the Valley of the Sun is Mormonism. The city of Mesa, formerly named Mesa City, was settled by Mormons from Utah and Idaho in 1878, and currently has the second largest Mormon population in the United States.[3] Mesa's massive Mormon Arizona Temple, which draws thousands of visitors every year, is a natural representation of this deceptive stronghold's spiritual rulership over Greater Phoenix.

Although most Mormons are very moral, considerate, devoted and family oriented people, the doctrinal foundation on which their entire belief system is built is grounded in heresy (Galatians 1:6-9, II Corinthians 11:4).

> Galatians 1:8   "But even if we, or an angel from heaven, preach any other gospel to you than what we have preached to you, let him be accursed."

> Proverbs 30:5,6   "Every word of God is pure; He is a shield to those who put their trust in Him. Do not add to His words, lest He reprove you, and you be found a liar."

Written by Joseph Smith, the Book of Mormon contradicts the Bible, proclaims "another gospel", and according to Holy Scripture must be rejected as an abomination.

Mormonism's doctrine of God maintains that:

•   The Father God is simply a man who achieved god-hood (*History of the Church*, V.6, p. 305).
•   God the Father has Eternal Wives through whom spirit children have been and continue to be born (*Mormon Doctrine*, 1966, p. 516; *The Seer*, Orson Pratt, p. 37, 158.).

•   Satan [Lucifer] was originally the spirit brother of Christ (*The Gospel Through the Ages*, p. 15).

Mormonism's doctrine of man asserts that:

•   Each person's essence, his intelligence, has always existed and so was never created (*Journal of Discourses*, X, p.5; VI, p. 6; *The Plan of Salvation*, p. 3; *Doctrine and Covenants*, 93.29).

•   Each person's spiritual body that clothed his intelligence in the pre-existent state was formed by the sexual union of the Father and one of His spirit wives (*The Seer*, Orson Pratt, p. 37).

•   Man has the potential of becoming God, just as Christ did; man is king of kings and lord of lords in embryo (*Times and Seasons*, August 1, 1844; *Journal of Discourses*, V. 10, p. 223; *History of the Church*, V. 6, p. 306; *Doctrine and Covenants*, 132.20).

Mormonism's doctrine of salvation affirms that:

•   Christ's blood shed on the cross only provides for the universal resurrection of all people and does not pay for personal sin (*Third Article of Faith*; *Journal of Discourses*, v. 3, p. 247; *Mormon Doctrine*, pp. 62, 669).

•   Christ's "blood" shed in the Garden of Gethsemane atones for most personal sin (*Church News*, Oct. 9, 1982, p. 19).

• The Church of Jesus Christ of Latter-day Saints (Mormons) restored the true gospel to the earth through Joseph Smith, and the true gospel is found only in it today (*Mormon Doctrine*, p. 334; *Teachings of the Prophet Joseph Smith*, p. 119).

• Salvation comes through a combination of faith, baptism in the church, and works (*Mormon Doctrine*, pp. 669-70; *Ensign*, Nov. 1982, p. 61).

• Eternal life (the power to attain godhood and have children in heaven) can only be achieved through obedience to the Mormon church and having one's marriage sealed in a Temple ceremony by the Mormon priesthood (*Journal of Discourses*, V. 11, p.221, 269; *Mormon Doctrine*, p. 411).

Not only does Mormonism violate the most fundamental of Bible doctrines, its founder, Joseph Smith, was an occultist and Mason (I Timothy 4:1-3).

Mormonism, Masonry, and Magic

The evidence of Joseph Smith's close connection to occultism and Freemasonry, and how this influenced the origin and development of the LDS Church is not widely known. Nevertheless, through the years, historians have documented a continuity between Joseph Smith's early occult practices and the origins of Mormonism, including the development of the LDS Temple ceremony.[4]

Through 1826, Joseph Smith and his father were involved in the occult practice known as "money digging". This involved special rituals and ceremonies which were performed for the purpose of obtaining buried treasure thought to be guarded by evil spirits. Smith's role in their endeavor was critical in that he utilized a brown "seer stone" through which he claimed that he could see supernaturally.[5]

On March 20, 1826, Smith was arrested, brought before a judge, and charged with being a "glass-looker" and disorderly person. At that time, a disorderly person was defined as someone who pretended to have skill in palmistry, fortune telling or discovering where lost goods might be found. Smith supposedly used this same "seer stone" to discover in 1827 and translate in 1829 the golden plates from which came the Book of Mormon.[6]

The following are representative of but a few of the essential characteristics common to both occult rituals and Mormon Temple ceremonies:

• They place an emphasis on the worthiness of initiates.

• They emphasize vows of secrecy.

• They feature prominent use of the sun, moon, and stars as key symbols.

• The purpose of the ritual is to assist mortals to attain to godhood.

Historian D. Michael Quinn concludes, "The Mormon endowment reflects the ancient and occult mysteries far closer than Freemasonry."[7]

Masonry's influence on Joseph Smith and the origins of Mormonism have been noted by numerous historians. Some of the areas impacted by Masonic lore and ritual include the Book of Mormon, Smith's personal life, and the LDS temple ceremony.[8]

For instance, Smith's so-called discovery of the gold plates mirrors the Enoch myth of Royal Arch Freemasonry, in which the prophet Enoch, instructed by a vision, preserved the Masonic mysteries by carving them on a golden plate that he placed in an arched stone vault marked with pillars to be rediscovered by Solomon. In the years to come, Enoch played a central role in Smith's emerging cosmology.[9]

Joseph Smith, his brother Hyrum, and many of their Mormon followers were Masons. The Mormon ceremony which came to be known as the Endowment, introduced by Joseph Smith to Mormon Masons, had an immediate inspiration from Masonry. In addition, the Mormon Nauvoo Temple constructed by Smith utilized numerous Masonic symbols and motifs.[10]

LDS historian Dr. Reed Durham concludes, "Many parallels found between early Mormonism and the Masonry of that day are substantial. There are few significant developments in the Church that occurred after March 15, 1842, which did not have some Masonic interdependence. The entire institution of the political kingdom of God, including the Council of Fifty, the living constitution, the proposed flag of the kingdom, and the anointing and coronation of the king, had its genesis in connection with Masonic thoughts and ceremonies. It appears that the prophet first embraced Masonry, and then in the process he modified, expanded, amplified, or glorified it."[11]

It is beyond the scope of this book to describe in detail Freemasonry's direct link to the occult. Nevertheless, it is evident that Mormonism is a cult and Joseph Smith, a false apostle.

II Corinthians 11:13 "For such are false apostles, deceitful workers, transforming themselves into apostles of Christ. And no wonder! For Satan himself transforms himself into an angel of light."

The appeal of Mormonism is great in the Valley of the Sun, not because of their doctrine, but because of their traditional emphasis on morality, family values, and community living. Many are willing to overlook Mormonism's doctrinal inconsistencies with the Bible in favor of family-oriented, relationship-based fellowship. In fact 75% of Mormon converts are from Christian churches.[12] Although Mormons are a moral people, they rally under a banner of deception and have grown into a massive constituency in the Valley of the Sun.

Counterfeit Callings and Perverted Purposes

The New Age, Mormonism, Freemasonry, and the occult are all forms of divination that have served to deceive many throughout Greater Phoenix. Like tares in a field of wheat, the enemy sows counterfeits alongside the genuine seeds that the Lord has planted. The Lord's planting will always foster the fulfillment of His ultimate purposes, whereas Satan's imitations deceptively misdirect and pervert the use of divinely disposed gifts in an effort to thwart the plans of God.

For example, a musical gift, bestowed by the Lord, may be used to further the kingdom of darkness instead of glorifying God, if Satan can successfully blind the person with the gift from the light of the knowledge of the saving power of Christ.

As we have discussed in this chapter, Satan not only seeks to deceive individuals, but also sows deception on a larger scale to beguile the masses. Knowing that Christ's redemptive calling upon the Valley of the Sun is to restore purpose to multitudes who have lost hope, Satan, through various forms of divination, has deceived thousands into pursuing perverted purposes.

Identifying these sources of divination in the Valley of the Sun is important. Nevertheless, we must not stop here, but press on to discover the effects of this spirit of divination, and the measures that must be taken to pull down this spiritual stronghold. It is also important that we understand, embrace and encourage the operation of the

75

genuine prophetic gifts of God, which are crucial to building divine purpose within the hearts of the multitudes that are continuing to flood the Valley of the Sun in search of their destiny.

Chapter 8

Trampling Serpents

An account in the book of Acts in the New Testament gives us greater insight into and understanding of the operation and effects of the spirit of divination (Acts 16:16-34). Having been commissioned by God to preach the gospel in Macedonia, Paul traveled with Silas to Philippi, the principal city of Macedonia (Acts 16:9-12). There they met "a slave girl, possessed with a spirit of divination, who brought her masters much profit through fortune telling". The literal Greek translation of the word divination in this passage is "puthon", from which we get the word python.

The Spirit of Python

The operation of this spirit of divination or python can be understood by observing how the python snake kills its prey. The python does not bite its victim, but instead slyly and slowly wraps itself around it. Before the victim realizes what has happened, it is in a death grip struggling for its very breath and life. The spirit of python operates in very much the same way, slowly squeezing the life out of its victim, whether it be a person, church or an entire city or nation.

When demonic powers are exposed, "all hell breaks loose" in the form of persecutions and tribulation. When the spirit of divination was cast out of the slave girl by the Apostle Paul, the multitude rose up against him and Silas and they were beaten violently and thrown into prison (Acts 16:18-24). Paul, recognizing the spirit of divination in the slave girl, also uncovered the stronghold over the city of Philippi that was prohibiting the gospel from being received. Nevertheless, Paul and Silas, while in prison, illustrated an effective tool in combating and defeating the spirit of divination or python.

Acts 16:25 "But at midnight Paul and Silas were praying and singing hymns to God, and the prisoners were listening to them."

Under the direction and anointing of the Holy Spirit, believers today can also be granted the authority to execute judgment on these same demonic kings and princes of the air, including the spirit of divination (Psalm 149:5-9).

Suddenly, a great earthquake shook the foundation of the prison and the chains that bound the apostles were loosed. The keeper of the prison, awakened by the earthquake, fell down trembling before the apostles and said, "Sirs, what must I do to be saved?" Paul and Silas then shared the gospel with the jail keeper and his entire household, and they were all saved and baptized that very night (Acts 16:26-34).

The unusual circumstances surrounding the salvation of the jail keeper and his household uncovers for us the greatest effect that the spirit of divination or python has upon mankind. The jailer literally begged the apostles to show him how to be saved from his sins, indicating that there was something previously preventing him from repenting and receiving the gospel. That something was a spirit of divination. Python was inhibiting the power and life of the gospel to reach the jailer and the people of Philippi. Once the power grip of python was broken by Paul and Silas, that region was at liberty to receive the gospel.

Divination Deters Repentance

The primary role and goal of the spirit of divination is to stop spiritual revival. Since repentance must precede true revival, python accomplishes this goal by preventing repentance from being wrought in believers and sinners alike.

In Old Testament times, false prophets, under the inspiration of a spirit of divination, falsely prophesied concerning Israel's and Judah's "peace" with a God who overlooked sin and the future "safety" of their nations. The majority, who believed these false prophets, caused the whole nation to turn away from the Lord and as a result reaped the judgment of God (Jeremiah 6:13-15).

> Jeremiah 23:16-17   Thus says the Lord of hosts: "Do not listen to the words of the prophets who prophesy to you. They make you worthless. They speak a vision of their own heart, not from the mouth of the Lord. They continually say to those who despise Me, 'The Lord has said, "You shall have peace"'; and to everyone who walks according to the imagination of his own heart, 'No evil shall come upon you.'"

Prophecy is a very powerful gift that is used to edify, exhort, comfort, bring direction and initiate repentance in individuals, churches, cities and nations (I Corinthians 14:1-5,39). However, when divination, Satan's counterfeit of the genuine prophetic gift, is in operation it produces deception and rebellion.

> Jeremiah 23:21,22   "I have not sent these prophets, yet they ran. I have not spoken to them, yet they prophesied. But if they had stood in My counsel, and had caused My people to hear My words, then **they would have turned them from their evil way** and from the evil of their doings."

Lamentations 2:14 "Your prophets have seen for you false and deceptive visions. **They have not uncovered your iniquity**, to bring back your captives, but have envisioned for you false prophecies and delusions."

Genuine prophecy will uncover sin and spark repentance, whereas false prophecy or divination will cause people to continue in and cover their sin. When complacent Christians, deluded by false prophecies of peace and safety, refuse to repent, the possibility of spiritual revival becomes almost nonexistent.

Since the spirit of divination is such a powerful tool of Satan in deterring repentance and revival, God's judgment is very harsh upon those who cooperate with this spirit. In the Old Testament, those who operated in divination were put to death (Deuteronomy 18:10-12).

Leviticus 20:27 "A man or a woman who is a medium, or who has familiar spirits, shall surely be put to death; they shall stone them with stones. Their blood shall be upon them."

Even King Saul fell under God's judgment of death, because he consulted a medium for direction. His disobedience with regard to mediums disqualified him from continued service in the kingdom of God.

I Chronicles 10:13,14 "So Saul died for his unfaithfulness which he had committed against the Lord, because he did not keep the word of the Lord, and also because he consulted a medium for guidance. But he did not inquire of the Lord; therefore He killed him, and turned the kingdom over to David the son of Jesse."

The judgment of the Lord upon diviners and false prophets, illustrated in the New Testament, is not quite as severe, since believers have the Holy Scriptures and indwelling Holy Spirit to assist them in judging prophetic utterance. In contrast, those of the Old Testament primarily had to rely on the word of the prophet when it came to knowing the will and direction of the Lord.

In the thirteenth chapter of the book of Acts, Paul and Barnabas encountered on the island of Paphos a Jewish sorcerer or false prophet by the name of Bar-Jesus. Sergius Paulus, the proconsul of the island, sought to hear the word of God that the apostles were bringing (Acts 13:6,7). However, when Bar-Jesus, under a spirit of divination, sought to turn the proconsul away from the faith, Paul rebuked him and pronounced a judgment of blindness upon him (Acts 13:8-11).

> Acts 13:11   "'And now, indeed, the hand of the Lord is upon you, and you shall be blind, not seeing the sun for a time.' And immediately a dark mist fell on him, and he went around seeking someone to lead him by the hand."

Witnessing the judgment of God through this sign, the proconsul believed the teaching of the Lord (Acts 13:12). This type of judgment from the Lord upon the mediums, psychics and false prophets who are deceiving, deluding and disqualifying people will become prevalent in the future, as the Lord's glory and anointing increases on the prophets of God.

Divination's Defilement

The spirit of divination not only deters repentance, but also brings defilement. According to Webster's Dictionary, defilement means "to make unclean or impure; to corrupt the purity or perfection of; to violate the sanctity of; desecrate, dishonor or contaminate."

> Leviticus 19:31   "Give no regard to mediums and familiar spirits; do not seek after them, to be defiled by them: I am the Lord your God."

In order for one to freely commune and fellowship with God in an intimate fashion, one must be holy and free from the stain of sin. By preventing repentance, the spirit of divination keeps people in an unholy and defiled state. As a result, intimate fellowship with God is impossible and revival fires are quenched.

> Leviticus 20:6,7   "And the person who turns after mediums and familiar spirits, to prostitute himself with them, I will set My face against that person and cut him off from his people. Sanctify yourselves therefore, and be holy, for I am the Lord your God."

Divination is an enemy of the holiness of God. Therefore, those corrupted by divination are disqualified and cut off from the move of God's Spirit.

Setting the Mark Through Prophetic Ministry

Paul's triumph over the stronghold of divination in Phillipi has set a scriptural precedent for the Church. Through the fervent, united, sustained, corporate intercessions and prophetic praises of the Church in the Valley of the Sun, the pulling down of the strongholds of divination over Greater Phoenix can become a reality.

Nevertheless, divination's defeat only becomes secure when the prophetic purposes of God are being proclaimed and performed. Without the prophetic revelation and proclamation of our purpose, calling and destiny, it is

82

easy to slip back into deception and complacency. For instance, although the city of Philippi was liberated from a stronghold of divination to receive the life-saving gospel, Paul took time to teach the Philippians concerning the importance of pursuing one's divine purpose, calling and destiny.

In his epistle to the Philippian church, the Apostle Paul made the following affirmation, "I press toward the mark for the prize of the high calling of God in Christ Jesus" (Philippians 3:14). Our pursuit of the Lord and His high calling for our lives is of paramount importance. Nevertheless, before we can press toward the mark of our high calling, the mark must first be set. For example, before a runner can win a race, he must know where the finish line is.

Without the setting of a mark or goal for our lives, we become aimless and unfruitful. When purpose fades and hope is lost, our reason for living dissolves. Death experienced on the inside breeds death in every area of our lives (Proverbs 17:22; 18:14).

Proverbs 13:12   "Hope deferred makes the heart sick, but when the desire comes it is a tree of life."

Although Scripture lays a foundation from which the Lord can build purpose in our lives, the Lord has set in the Church prophetic ministry gifts to assist us in planning for and framing our future. Throughout history, the Lord has anointed prophets to proclaim the will and purpose of God for individuals, cities and nations.

Of the nine gifts of the Spirit mentioned in Apostle Paul's first epistle to the Corinthian church, the one gift he encouraged them to earnestly desire was prophecy (I Corinthians 14:1,39). Paul emphasized the practice of prophetic ministry because it can supply vision, provide purpose, define destiny and create hope like no other spiritual gift (I Corinthians 14:31). A divinely inspired personal prophecy enables one to remain focused and determined to reach their mark, despite hurdles and roadblocks (I Corinthians 14:3).

> I Timothy 1:18 "This charge I commit to you, son Timothy, according to the prophecies previously made concerning you, that by them you may wage the good warfare."

Since a major component of the Valley of the Sun's redemptive calling is to plant purpose in people, the Lord has ordained Greater Phoenix to be a refuge wherein the prophetic word can freely be administered and received by those in need of a future and a hope (Jeremiah 29:11). Nevertheless, Phoenician church history bears out that Satan has made it his goal to either drive out, discredit or destroy every genuine prophetic gift that the Lord has sought to establish in the Valley of the Sun.

Crushing Satan Underneath Our Feet

Crushing Satan underneath our feet is neither our ultimate goal nor primary reason for rejoicing. We plunder Satan's camp so that we can fulfill the purpose of God for our generation.

> Luke 10:19,20 "Behold, I give you the authority to **trample on serpents and scorpions**, and over all the power of the enemy, and nothing shall by any means hurt you. Nevertheless, do not rejoice in this, that the spirits are subject to you, but rather rejoice because your names are written in heaven."

Receiving Christ as our personal Savior and Lord is the first step on a long road to our divine destination. Although having our names written in heaven is a marvelous thing, we must not terminate our journey after the first step. Instead, we must be determined to press forward toward our divine destiny, so that not only our names but also our prayers and righteous deeds are recorded in heaven's annals for all to read throughout eternity.

Greater Phoenix is destined by God to be an oasis of new hope, wherein the prophetic gift sets destiny's mark for multitudes. Let us therefore endeavor to embrace, encourage, and develop the genuine prophetic gifts the Lord is raising up in the Valley of the Sun.

Chapter 9

The Sting of Rejection

God builds on purpose and with people, while Satan destroys with deception and through division. Understanding Satan's deceptive devices in distracting thousands in the Valley of the Sun from pursuing their divine destiny, let us now uncover the wiles Satan has been using to divide and isolate Greater Phoenix's growing multitude.

Settlers Came to Stake Their Claim

No matter how clearly defined our purpose in God is, without the interaction and cooperation of other people, we will never fulfill our divine destiny. Knowing this, Satan, throughout the ages, has devised schemes to strategically divide and destroy people.

> Matthew 12:25 "Every kingdom divided against itself is brought to desolation, and every city or house divided against itself will not stand."

The selfish and covetous pursuit of possessions, prestige and power provides a platform from which Satan can build dividing walls between people (I Timothy 6:10).

> I John 2:16 "For all that is in the world - the lust of the flesh, the lust of the eyes, and the pride of life - is not of the Father but is of the world."

Arizona was one of the final frontiers in the United States to be settled. Therefore, in the late 1800s, many prospectors, settlers, farmers and businessmen in search of fame, fortune and a future staked their claims in the Valley of the Sun.

86

The competitive nature of the settler's pursuits fostered insecurities that produced in them haughty attitudes of superiority. Prevalent among the Hohokam before them, the elitist attitudes that many Phoenician settlers adopted caused them to exclude newcomers and suppress surrounding resident people groups. These elitist attitudes, which prevail today throughout the Valley of the Sun, span every venue of life including the Church. The result is an atmosphere wherein elitism rules and rejection reigns.

Racism, Rejection and Segregation

Unlike El Paso, Albuquerque, and Tucson, Phoenix from its founding was run by Anglos for Anglos at the great expense of other races.[1] Indeed, Phoenician history clearly illustrates the rejection and suppression of African Americans, Hispanics, Chinese, and the Japanese by the Anglo-supremacist establishment.

In March 1909, Arizona's Territorial Legislature passed a proposal allowing Arizona school districts to segregate students of African ancestry from students of other racial backgrounds. Although few districts in Arizona adopted segregation between African Americans and whites in schools, Phoenix did so in April 1910, despite the valiant opposition of Arizona Governor Joseph H. Kibbey, Booker T. Washington, William P. Crump, and Samuel F. Bayless. In 1912, the prevailing racist attitude of white Phoenicians toward African Americans is captured by the following recorded remarks. The Afro-American Club in Phoenix is "a moral sink", a "vehicle for the exercise of license and debauchery", a "lawless nigger club", and a "disgrace to the city of Phoenix."[2] Anglo-Phoenician attitudes toward and accommodations for African Americans into the mid 1920's were no better. One author noted, "Segregated from the Anglo community in restaurants, theaters, hospitals, hotels, swimming pools, buses, and other public places, blacks were viewed by white Phoenicians as second-class citizens."[3]   Racist attitudes towards African Americans have continued into the 1990s, as Arizona for years refused to observe the Martin Luther King, Jr., national holiday, and only recently has adopted it.

Similarly, the Hispanic population, which constitutes the largest minority in the Valley of the Sun, incurred the sting of Anglo-Phoenician rejection.   One observer noted, "Often shut out of the larger community, Mexicans created their own social and cultural life centered around family activities at home and religious services. Patterns of discrimination and segregation encouraged the development of the Phoenix Mexican community."[4]

Like other racial minority groups, the Chinese were encouraged by the white population to seek refuge in their own neighborhood. As a result, Chinatown became the most tightly knit ethnic community in Phoenix. After an interview with Chinatown leader Ong Dick in 1911, black leader Booker T. Washington commented, "The Chinaman is an alien in this country. I doubt whether any other portion of the population remains so thoroughly foreign as is true of the Chinaman."[5]

In 1921, state legislation enacted the Arizona Alien Land Law which forbade Japanese aliens the right to "acquire, possess, enjoy, transmit, and inherit real property or interest therein." However, not until 1934, during the Great Depression, did militant white farmers organize the Anti-Alien Association in an effort to strictly enforce the law. As a result, Japanese farms were damaged and destroyed, and Japanese farmers were harassed and attacked.   The Anti-Alien Association, which soon had hundreds of members, organized "anti-Jap" motorcades to drive through the valley to protest the "Yellow Peril" and to demand the removal of "the Japs" from Arizona. This crisis established

Phoenix as a focal point of racial prejudice and discrimination against the Japanese that contributed to the breakdown of Japanese-American relations that eventually led to World War II.[6] During World War II, the War Relocation Authority mandated that members of the Japanese population in Phoenix be sent to the Colorado and Gila River Relocation Centers, which were located respectively near the Arizona towns of Poston and Rivers. Over 30,000 Japanese suffered over a four year period in these two fenced concentration camps.[7]

Apache Atrocities

Despite the rejection and injustices that other minorities endured, no other people group has suffered under the reign of Arizonian Anglo-supremacist settlers more than Native Americans.

Apache raids of Mexico that continued after the Mexican War (1846-1848) prompted the U.S. to establish various camps, forts and posts throughout central Arizona in an attempt to control Apache activity.[8] Although the Apaches were not innocent of wrongdoing in many incidents with U.S. settlers, the following events which occurred near modern-day Phoenix greatly contributed to the estrangement, isolation, deportation and demoralization of the Apache Indians.

In January 1864, an American expedition of civilians out of Prescott, led by King Woosley, requested a meeting with Apache leaders near modern day Globe. Six Apache leaders responded, and after all were seated, Woosley signaled his men to kill every Apache possible. So many Apaches were killed that the stream where the massacre took place ran red with the blood and was called "Bloody Tanks".[9]

In the Spring of 1871, five hundred Apaches came to Camp Grant, near modern day San Manuel, seeking peace with the white man. Sympathetic to the Apaches difficult circumstances, the camp's young commander, Royal E. Whitman, befriended the Apaches and their chief, Eskiminzin. However, on April 30, 1871, a group of men from Tucson treacherously attacked this sleeping, peace-seeking Apache camp, killing 144, the majority of which were women and children. Unfortunately, all perpetrators of this crime were acquitted in a trial later that year, and one of the principal leaders of the attack, Sidney De Long, was later elected mayor of Tucson. This incident, known as the "Camp Grant Massacre", forever stained relations between Apaches and the white man.[10]

Although a measure of peace and agreement between the Apache and U.S. resulted in the establishment of the San Carlos Apache Indian Reservation in December 1872, Tonto Apache and Yavapai relations were still hostile. Ensuing battles resulted in the slaughter of seventy six Yavapai Indians at "Skull Cave" near modern day Canyon Lake on December 28, 1872, and the butchery of fifty Yavapai Indians at "Turret Peak" near modern day Cordes Junction on March 6, 1873.[11]

Although the resistance of most Apaches and Yavapais ceased by 1873, their plight continued. In 1875, all Apache Indians in Arizona were transferred from other reservations to the San Carlos Reservation. In one instance, 1500 Apache and Yavapai Indians were forced to walk over 100 miles in the dead of winter from the Fort Verde Reservation to the San Carlos Reservation. At least twenty-five children were born on this trail and one old man had carried his invalid wife in a basket on his back the entire distance.[12]

In the spring of 1877, even Geronimo, the heroic Chiricahua Apache, was brought in chains to the San Car-

90

los Reservation. Geronimo and his band in subsequent years repeatedly escaped the reservation only to be recaptured and returned again. On September 4, 1886, Geronimo and his band were captured for the last time at Skeleton Canyon. They were then shipped on a train along with peaceful Chiricahua Apaches to St. Augustine, Florida and put to hard labor "to teach them all a lesson". There many Chiricahuas died from malaria or tuberculosis. In 1894, the Chiricahuas were sent to Fort Sill, Oklahoma, where Geronimo died in 1909.[13]

Phoenix and the Indians

Phoenix is the only major city in the Southwest with no modern Indian heritage. The Hohokam Indians (300 B.C. – 1450 A.D.) had vacated the Salt River Valley long before Phoenix was established in the 1800s. Since Phoenix was founded by whites at a much later date than Los Angeles, El Paso, Albuquerque, and Tucson, it had no native population. Nevertheless, a large native Pima and Maricopa Indian population surrounded Phoenix. Diminishing water resources on the Gila River reservation drove the Pimas and Maricopa Indians north to the Salt River Valley.[14]

These native immigrants, who simply sought to farm in peace in the Valley of the Sun, were unwelcomed by Anglo-Phoenicians. In an attempt to contain displaced Pima Indians and restrain them from frequenting the city, the Salt River Reservation was established just east of Phoenix in 1879. In 1881, a city ordinance was passed requiring all Indians, unless employed by a white resident, to leave the city at sundown.[15]

As Phoenix's economy grew, the demand for cheap labor increased dramatically. Therefore, Phoenix promoters along with the Indian Bureau established the Phoenix

Indian School on September 3, 1891. The Indian School's "outing system" sent school children into the community to work as domestic servants and laborers. Due to the growing demand for laborers, in 1923, the Indian Bureau established a relocation program through the Indian School to "colonize" Phoenix with reservation Indians. By 1925, through this program, about 400 Indians were added to Phoenix's work force.[16]

Phoenician discrimination of Indians was not as intense as with other minority groups since they brought visible economic benefits to the city, were few in number, and never grouped together in a specific neighborhood. Nevertheless, the primary reason for Anglo-Phoenician tolerance of Indians was that they neither engaged in political activities nor threatened the economic interests of whites who sought to establish and build their kingdoms in the Valley of the Sun. One author wrote, "Phoenicians seemed to consider the Indians a harmless nuisance."[17]

Crippled By Scorpion's Sting

The paralyzing effects of rejection are akin to those of the scorpion, whose stealth sting immobilizes its victim.[18] Oftentimes, the severity of scorpion's sting cannot be accurately assessed until its crippling effects manifest over generations. The abuse, abandonment and betrayal that the American Indian incurred at the hands of Anglo supremacists has proven to be more devastating than that of any other people group in the United States, including African Americans.

Currently, the unemployment rate on most Indian reservations is about 50%, compared to 4% in the U.S. as a whole. The suicide rate for American Indians is five times higher than any other ethnic group. A 1995 study found that 26.5% of deaths for Indian men were linked to alcohol, which is 5.6 times the overall U.S. rate. Currently, 31.6% of American Indians live below the poverty line, compared with 13% for the entire U.S.[19] The American Indian average life expectancy is 40.9 years for men and 46 for women. The school dropout rate is three times the national average and the infant mortality is double the national rate.[20]

American Anglo's ostracism of American Indians has estranged Indians not only from the white man, but also from the white man's God. Although 8% of American Indians have aligned themselves with Christianity in some way, Native pastors claim that less than 1% are truly born again.[21]

Proverbs 18:19   "A brother offended is harder to win than a strong city."

The effects of rejection upon the multitudes, including bitterness and hopelessness, have their origins in covert demonic activity. Knowing that a major component of Christ's redemptive purpose for the Greater Phoenix area is to renew hope, plant purpose, and impart destiny within the hearts of multitudes, Satan has strategically established demonic strongholds in the Valley of the Sun that have caused an undeniable pattern of rejection among residents, resulting in the despair and isolation of hundreds of thousands of "would be", Spirit united, Christian soldiers.

In addition to providing God's prescription for healing the wounds inflicted by the sting of rejection, in the following chapter we will also specifically identify the spirits of darkness responsible for rejection's sting and provide a Biblical battle plan to crush them underneath our feet.

Chapter 10

Treading on Scorpions

Fear allows spirits of bondage to enslave us, keeping us from attaining our high calling in Christ Jesus (Romans 8:15, Philippians 3:14). As was briefly discussed in the previous chapter, the selfish ambition of Phoenician claim-staking settlers fostered a competitive atmosphere in which insecurities arose whenever newcomers threatened settlers' positions in the community. Settlers' fears allowed a spirit of bondage, namely jealousy, to operate through them, causing them to reject newcomers and suppress native people groups.

Over the years, jealousy has so bound much of the Greater Phoenix establishment that it has become one of the most powerful spiritual strongholds in the Valley of the Sun. As a result, many that have been sovereignly directed to come to Phoenix for a new start are immediately faced with rejection in one form or another. Unfortunately, many of those who come to Phoenix in search of new life and purpose are in such a weakened condition when they arrive that they perish under the sting of rejection. Some become embittered by jealousy themselves. Others surrender to grief and either isolate themselves, return to where they came from, or find refuge and acceptance among family oriented Mormons, or fraternal organizations like the Masons.

The Fear of Rejection

The fear of rejection is the source of many spiritual diseases that ensnare the hearts of multitudes in the Valley of the Sun. We all have been rejected at some time by someone in our lives, or have been unjustly denied certain

94

privileges or rewards that rightfully belonged to us. For some of us it may have been facing the rejection of a parent who favored another sibling, losing out on a job opportunity to a less qualified individual, enduring divorce to a beloved yet unfaithful spouse, experiencing the betrayal of a close friend, or being shunned for upholding an unpopular point of view.

Rejection results from one being denied love. When one is truly loved, he is unconditionally accepted and eternally adopted. On the other hand, when one is rejected, he is disapproved and refused. Rejection manifests in different forms and can result from being abandoned, avoided, betrayed, denied, deserted, disapproved, disregarded, excluded, ignored, neglected, ostracized, rebuffed, repelled, ridiculed, scorned, shunned, slighted, spurned or turned down.

The Father builds His kingdom on love and unconditional acceptance, whereas Satan seeks to divide the Father's kingdom through rejection. Those who are secure in the Father's love and acceptance can flourish in the kingdom without the approval of men.

> John 6:37   "All that the Father gives Me will come to Me, and the one who comes to Me I will by no means cast out."

> Ephesians 1:5, 6   ". . . having predestined us to adoption as sons by Jesus Christ . . . He has made us accepted in the Beloved."

When one truly walks with God, the Father's love is shed abroad in their hearts by the Spirit of adoption, which is the Holy Spirit. Nothing in this world, especially mankind, can separate them from the love and acceptance of the Father.

Romans 8: 15 "For you did not receive the **spirit of bondage** again to fear, but you received the **Spirit of adoption** by whom we cry out, 'Abba, Father'."

Jesus Himself was "despised and rejected by men and we did not esteem Him" (Isaiah 53:3). Yet, His spiritual reaction to rejection empowered Him to obey and fulfill His heavenly calling. Jesus was secure in the Father's love and did not require the acceptance of men. Jesus was not a man pleaser. On the contrary, Jesus "did not receive honor from men" and rebuked the Jews for seeking honor from one another instead of from God (John 5:41-44).

Those whom we fear and reverence we also will honor and love. Our fear of God is evidenced by our honor and love for Him. However, if we fear man, we will seek the honor and acceptance of men above the honor of God. Those who fear the rejection of men are subject to spirits of bondage.

It is Satan's goal to completely immobilize sinners and saints alike in the Valley of the Sun through rejection's scorpion-like sting. Carnal reactions to rejection open the door for demonization and a life of spiritual incarceration. The fear of rejection chains many Phoenicians to the destiny's starting blocks, disabling them from even beginning the race towards the mark for the prize of the high calling of God in Christ Jesus.

Proverbs 29:25 "The fear of man brings a snare."

The sting of rejection is inevitable in this life. Unfortunately, many fear being rejected and react carnally when ignored, neglected or disapproved. Rejection is a root problem that has served to hinder many Christians in the Valley of the Sun from uniting with and taking an ef-

fective role in the corporate Body of Christ in Greater
Phoenix.

The Bitter Root of Jealousy

One common carnal reaction to rejection's sting is
bitterness and unforgiveness, which flourishes in a rebellious heart of pride. Pride, which does not allow self to be
"knocked down", promotes and esteems self over others.
Those who carnally react to rejection in this manner defend
their position by becoming critical of others, working diligently to compete for the approval of God and man. Unfortunately, those in this condition become vulnerable to a
spirit of jealousy. Pride blinds them of their own jealousy,
resulting in a deep self-deception that leads to a hardened,
unrepentant heart, shipwrecked faith and an unfulfilled divine destiny.

Obadiah 3   "The pride of your heart has deceived
you."

Jeremiah 17:9,10   "The heart is deceitful above all
things, and desperately wicked; Who can know it?
I, the Lord, search the heart, I test the most secret
parts, even to give every man according to his ways,
and according to the fruit of his doings."

Jealousy is a deceptive, destructive and divisive
spirit that works not only in high places, but also in secret
places, hiding from its victim in the inner recesses of their
heart (Ezekiel 8:3-6). Jealousy works in one a sense of un-
easiness or anxiety that stems from the fear of preference
being given to another. Criticism of and competition with
others are jealousy's fruit that has disqualified many in the
Valley of the Sun from effective service in the kingdom of
God (II Corinthians 10:12). Ultimately, the goal of the

97

spirit of jealousy is to keep believers deceived, embittered and divided.

There are numerous examples of jealousy in the Bible. In every case, a spirit of jealousy is entertained by an arrogant and rebellious heart that has been wounded through some form of rejection. For example, Joseph's brothers were jealous of the favor and honor he was receiving from their father Jacob. Their bitter resentment and jealousy compelled them to remove Joseph from their midst, an unrighteous deed that tormented them for many years (Genesis 37:3,4).

Likewise, Korah and his company were jealous of Moses' rank and position, and sought to promote themselves by taking matters into their own hands. Unfortunately, jealousy cost Korah and his men their very lives (Numbers 16:1-33).

In the New Testament, we find Simon the Sorcerer, who after becoming a Christian, was jealous of the apostles' power and the prestige they were receiving in his stead. After Simon offered Peter money to obtain spiritual gifts, Peter saw that Simon's heart was not right with God and realized he was bound and embittered by a jealous spirit. This heart condition disqualified Simon from receiving the anointing (Acts 8:18-23).

Ultimately, bitterness and jealousy grow into weeds that choke out the purpose that has been sown in us, defile the fruit that we are destined to bear, and bring division to the Body of Christ.

Intercession vs. Accusation

There are two ministries that function continuously. The first is the ministry of intercession, whose author is Jesus. The goal of intercession is to present every person perfect and complete before the Father, thereby nurturing and promoting unity and purity in the Body (Colossians 1:28, 29). Jesus, Who continually makes intercession for the saints, desires us to be transformed into His likeness in spirit, word and deed (Galatians 4:19). Therefore, He has called and destined the Church to be a house of prayer for all nations (Mark 11:17).

Hebrews 7:25 "He is also able to save to the uttermost those who come to God through Him, since He ever lives to make intercession for them."

The second perpetual ministry is the ministry of accusation, whose author is Satan (Revelation 12:10). Accusation serves to discourage, degrade and defame believers in order to generate dysfunction and disharmony among brethren. Those bound by a spirit of jealousy partake of the ministry of accusation through judgment and criticism of and comparison with other believers (James 4:11,12, Matthew 7:1,2).

Jealousy is a serious spiritual disease with grave consequences. Jealousy, which germinates and flourishes in a heart of pride, cost Satan his position in heaven (Ezekiel 28:14-17). Likewise, jealousy has caused many Christians in the Valley of the Sun to forfeit their spiritual rank in the army of God and remain in a spiritual wilderness.

In this hour, the unity of the Spirit throughout Greater Phoenix is vital for true revival and community transformation to take place. Therefore, the Lord will not anoint and appoint those bound by jealousy, since their spiritual malady and ministry of accusation generate strife and competition among the ranks and serve only to further divide the Body of Christ.

Joel 2:7,8   "They run like mighty men, they climb the wall like men of war; every one marches in formation, and they do not break ranks. They do not push one another; every one marches in his own column. And when they lunge between the weapons, they are not halted by losses."

We, the Church in the Valley of the Sun, must open our hearts in absolute surrender to the Master, that He might expose and extract any roots of bitterness and jealousy, that we might truly become ministers of reconciliation rather than agents of division.

Overcoming Jealousy

Jealousy finds its way into every facet of life, including the work place, school, the church and especially the home. Jealousy in marriage is probably one of the most potentially dangerous conditions that exist in our world today. Sometimes a marriage partner, who fears rejection by a mate, will resort to control tactics in an effort to eliminate any possibility of further rejection. Jealousy is a strong spirit that can result in murdering a mate, rather than dealing with the rejection of divorce or losing a mate to someone else.

Song of Solomon 8:6   "For love is as strong as death, **jealousy as cruel (severe) as the grave**; its flames are flames of fire, a most vehement flame."

If we will learn to react properly to rejection, we can overcome jealousy. Our spiritual reaction to rejection will bring us victory in life every time. The foundation for overcoming rejection is an experiential knowledge of the unconditional love and acceptance of God. Oftentimes, healing the wounds of rejection requires the tender, loving touch of another human being. Once love is received and a degree of trust is built, a jealous spirit can be overcome.

The first step on the road to healing from rejection and deliverance from jealousy is to humble oneself. God resists the proud in heart, but gives grace to the humble (James 4:6). Pride deceives the heart, whereas a humble spirit garners God's grace, granting repentance to the acknowledging of the truth (I Timothy 2:25,26).

As we acknowledge our embittered condition due to the rejection of the past, we then can be led to forgive those who have inflicted scorpion's sting. Repentance from bitterness, resentment and unforgiveness not only releases God's forgiveness, but also cleanses the spirit.

Repentance plays a very important role in the restoration process, loosening Satan's grip and providing a clear path to demonic deliverance. However, once deliverance from jealousy takes place, measures must be taken and new patterns established to maintain freedom from this demonic oppression. We must be determined to not only forgive past offenses, but also forget them. Later the enemy will most certainly attempt to reopen old wounds of rejection through different circumstances and people.

Though rejection can be very real and cruel, if our focus remains on the Father and His unconditional acceptance, we will not react carnally. Faith in God's love will always supplant the fear of rejection, and assure us of our special place in His heart. As we abide in Christ's love and partake of His meek and quiet spirit, we will find rest for our souls and know full well that He is faithful to promote us in His timing to fulfill our unique role in His kingdom (I Thessalonians 5:24).

How will we know when we are secure in His love and undaunted by rejection?

•   When we can humbly abide in the Spirit of adoption and be completely content in having only the Father's acceptance.

•   When we don't feel slighted when others are given more attention than ourselves.

•   When we can sincerely rejoice in the promotion of others, offering unfeigned words of encouragement.

•   When we can quickly forgive those who reject us and pray for those who spitefully use us for their gain.

•   When we can obey God without hesitation, despite the rejection and disapproval of family and close friends.

In this critical hour, we all must realize that the bitter root of jealousy will defile our spiritual fruit, keep us from walking in our high calling, and cause division in the Body of Christ. We therefore must cry out for the Lord's judgments concerning the secret faults of bitterness and jealousy, that we might not lose our reward.

The Hopelessness of Grief

The other carnal reaction to the sting of rejection is resignation, which has its origins in a heart of self-pity. Those who carnally react to rejection in this manner feel sorry for themselves and withdraw. They attempt to draw the attention and sympathy of others through their self-proclaimed hopeless condition.

In general, those who succumb to rejection are often caught up in self. These individuals are usually very introspective, and continually require prayer, counsel or ministry. Yet, they rarely consider the needs or desires of others and are takers by nature. They are referred to by some as "high maintenance, low impact" individuals.

Unfortunately, those who continue in this behavior pattern, become vulnerable to a spirit of grief. The sin of selfishness opens the door for demonization. When the spirit of grief takes hold, the once manipulative, attention-drawing behavior pattern can transform into uncontrollable depression. If not dealt with, the victim could fall into the dregs of despair, and be resigned into a quagmire of hope-lessness.

The spirit of grief often disguises itself as humility. Victims verbally undermine and demean themselves in an attempt to draw pity from others. Through this practice they deceive themselves and others into believing that they are a model of submission and meekness. However, the fruit of true humility, exemplified by Jesus, is self-sacrifice and unselfish service to others (Philippians 2:5-8, Mark 10:45). A spirit of grief, on the contrary, selfishly demands attention and expects service.

> Philippians 2:3,4   "Let nothing be done through selfish ambition or conceit, but in lowliness of mind let each esteem others better than himself. Let each of you look out not only for his own interests, but also for the interests of others."

Once deliverance from this condition is administered, a common way of assisting a person in walking out their de-liverance is to establish a pattern of service to others.

Escapism is a common response of those who have entertained a spirit of grief due to the sting of rejection. Escapism can manifest through day dreaming, excessive sleep, or drugs and alcohol. Another tell-tale sign is self-degradation and self-pity, where one severely undermines one's own abilities and worth. A more obvious behavior pattern of those bound by grief is withdrawal, where one avoids people, relationships and responsibilities. Often-times, victims unwittingly set themselves up to fail in relationships, thus creating a cycle of rejection. They seem bent on their own destruction, making a case against themselves. In severe cases, victims are subject to committing suicide, judging that their lives are hopeless and simply not worth living.

Recovering Our High Calling

The prophet Elijah serves as a solid Biblical example of how self-pity and the spirit of grief works to cause one to forfeit one's high calling in life. Elijah, who called fire down from heaven and executed the 450 prophets of Baal, was intimidated by the threats of the wicked queen Jezebel and found himself running for his life (I Kings 18, 19). Wearied by continual persecution and rejection, Elijah began feeling sorry for himself. He then entered into a wilderness where he pleaded to the Lord that he might die (I Kings 19:4). The Lord met him in his moment of weakness by sending an angel to strengthen him (I Kings 19:5-8).

Yet forty days after receiving strength and refreshing from the Lord, Elijah entered a cave of resignation. In self-pity, he complained to the Lord of being Israel's lone prophet. The Lord clearly asked Elijah what he was doing in the cave and why he was not performing the will of God. Although the Lord manifested Himself to Elijah in a strong wind and an earthquake, he didn't need those things to know God's will. As a prophet of the Lord, Elijah knew the still, small voice of the Master. He was simply unwilling to obey and wanted the Lord to join in on his pity party (I Kings 19:9-15). Finally the Lord could not continue on with Elijah's stubbornness, since the destiny of a nation was at stake. Therefore, He anointed and appointed Elisha to take Elijah's place.

104

I Kings 19:16   "And Elisha the son of Shaphat of
Abel Meholah you shall anoint as prophet in your
place."

In these last days, the Lord requires prompt obedience from His servants. He doesn't have 2000 years, and
many believe even 50 years to fulfill His mission in the
earth through His Church. Although the Lord's callings are
irrevocable, we can choose to forfeit the call of God on our
lives by submitting to self-pity and a spirit of grief. Despite our resignation from our high calling, we will be
judged by the Lord according to it at the judgment seat of
Christ.

Jesus Himself endured the greatest rejection that
could ever be imagined. Not only was He rejected of men,
but He also was for a moment rejected by His Father in
heaven (Psalm 22:6-8).

Psalms 22:1   "My God, My God, why have You
forsaken Me?"

However, Jesus' sacrifice on the cross gave Him all
authority and power over grief and sorrow, so that we do
not have to bear its burden.

Isaiah 53:3,4   "He is despised and rejected by men,
a Man of sorrows and acquainted with grief . . . and
we did not esteem Him. Surely He has borne our
griefs and carried our sorrows."

Therefore, let us never relinquish our calling and
anointing to another by succumbing to self-pity and grief.
Instead, let us repent of them, cast them on the shoulders of
Jesus, and pursue with godly zeal our high and holy calling
to the glory of God.

Rejected But Not Affected

The effects of the scorpion-like sting of rejection inflicted upon African Americans, Hispanic, Chinese, Japanese, Indians, and other people groups in the Valley of the Sun are widespread and prevalent. Indeed, the elitist attitudes of insecure, haughty spirited settlers have endured and produced a stronghold of racism and jealousy, resulting in the rejection and isolation of thousands in the Valley of the Sun. Nevertheless, the Lord's remedy for scorpion stings, if taken as prescribed in this chapter, will cause us as individuals to become immune to rejection. The following summarizes the spirits that influence carnal and spiritual reactions to rejection, along with the attitudes, fruit, words, and works that accompany them.

Carnal Reactions to Rejection

SPIRITS	Jealousy	Grief
ATTITUDES	Pride	Self-Pity
FRUIT	Bitterness	Hopelessness
WORDS	Criticism	Self-Degradation
WORKS	Competition	Resignation

Spiritual Reaction to Rejection

SPIRIT	Adoption
ATTITUDE	Humility
FRUIT	Contentment
WORDS	Encouragement
WORKS	Obedience

Repentance and Racial Reconciliation

Although we can enjoy immunity from the scorpion's sting of rejection as individuals, the remedy for rejection must also be administered on a corporate level for widespread healing to occur. In the Valley of the Sun and throughout Arizona, it is imperative that the Church continue to initiate repentance and racial reconciliation toward those people groups, especially the American Indians, whom we and our forefathers have rejected. Only then can we, as a corporate Body, be liberated from the curse and bondage of rejection and effectively trample scorpions underneath our feet (Luke 10:19).

Having defined Christ's redemptive purposes for Greater Phoenix and identified the demonic strongholds that seek to hinder their fulfillment, let's now discover the unique spiritual work that the Lord seeks to do in the 21st century Church in the Valley of the Sun. Since it is in the economy of God to affect the world through His Church, it is imperative that the Church in the Valley of the Sun understands and embraces the preparatory work that He needs to do in us. Only then can we through Christ positively affect and transform Greater Phoenix into the city of refuge it is destined to become.

Section III

The Sun of Righteousness Shall Arise With Healing In His Wings

Chapter 11

Unto Those Who Fear My Name

Divine callings and purposes are often defined by Biblical themes, characters or even specific Scriptures. For example, after the Lord miraculously healed Kenneth Hagin of a life threatening disease at age 16, he dedicated his entire life and ministry to teaching the Body of Christ faith principles based on the scripture passage, Mark 11:23,24. The Lord commissioned him by saying "Go teach My people faith". Kenneth Hagin later became one of the forerunners of the "Word of Faith" movement and founder of Rhema Bible College.

Individuals, churches, ministries, organizations, institutions and cities, if consecrated to the Lord, have an underlying, Biblical, redemptive theme that characterizes their mission. The preceding prophetic revelations in this book have helped identify the redemptive purpose of the Valley of the Sun. Now let us define more specifically the preparatory work that the Lord must perform in the Church before He can fulfill His purposes in the Valley of the Sun through the Church.

The Healing of a Nation

The Lord has foreordained certain cities in every nation to be "cities of refuge" wherein people can flock to first be healed, then empowered and finally commissioned to fulfill their divine destiny (Joshua 20). Phoenix is one of these "cities of refuge" wherein the healing of our nation will commence.

The redemptive purpose of Phoenix is captured in the last book of the Old Testament, which was written by the prophet Malachi. Malachi not only identified the overall condition of the end-time Church, but also provided a prophetic prescription for the healing of the Church and the nations. This medicine of the Spirit, if taken properly, will not only bring healing to the Church in the Valley of the Sun, but will also empower us to spearhead the healing of our nation.

The recent escalation of random acts of terrorism in America is a tell-tale symptom of an epidemic of rebellion that is spreading across our nation. This raging spirit of lawlessness is the product of multiplied thousands of hearts that have been poisoned through the sting of divorce, covetous lusts, idolatry and complacency among other things. If America, our "One Nation Under God", is in great need of healing, then what of our neighboring non-Christian nations, who must be plagued by an even greater stronghold of lawlessness?

The antidote for any plague is of course Jesus Christ, the Healer. However, the Lord has chosen to manifest His manifold wisdom and healing power through the Church (Ephesians 3:10). If the health of the Church in the Valley of the Sun is poor, Christ's power to heal through the Church here is greatly diminished. Therefore, the Lord must first address the Greater Phoenician Church about our condition before we can effectively minister to the multitudes flocking to the Valley of the Sun in search of refuge, healing and a new start.

Judgment in God's House

The prophet Malachi preached repentance to an indifferent Israel approximately 425 years before the coming of Christ. Malachi identified three specific arenas of sin which plagued Israel, namely, a corrupt priesthood that offered defiled offerings, the neglect of tithes and offerings, and divorce. Interestingly enough, this Old Covenant

112

prophet clearly identified the very sins that are plaguing the end-time Church.

> I Peter 4:17 For the time has come for judgment to begin at the house of God; and if it begins with us first, what will be the end of those who do not obey the gospel of God?"

Currently, as a whole, the Church is a royal priesthood that has lost its first love, and forsaken its sacrificial devotion to prayer and the presence of God (I Peter 2:9, Revelation 2:4). We have neglected to offer our bodies a living sacrifice unto God and as a result have conformed to this world's idolatrous pursuits of pleasure, becoming enemies instead of friends of God (Romans 12:1,2, James 4:4). In a nutshell, we have offered the Lord our worst fruits instead of our first fruits (Malachi 1:6-14).

> Malachi 1:7,8 "You offer defiled food on My altar by saying, 'The table of the Lord is contemptible.' And when you offer the lame and sick, is it not evil?"

In 1999, the divorce rate in the Church was 7% higher than the overall divorce rate in America.[1] Traditional Christian values including covenant marriages are being threatened with extinction as Christian marriages are being severed by the thousands, resulting in a total breakdown of the family unit. (Malachi 2:13-16).

> Malachi 2:14,16 "The Lord has been witness between you and the wife of your youth, with whom you have dealt treacherously. For the Lord God of Israel says that He hates divorce."

Less than 10% of American Christians practice tithing. Our thievery of the Most High God has opened the door for the devourer instead of opening the windows of heaven (Malachi 3:10).

> Malachi 3:8 "Will a man rob God? Yet you have robbed Me in tithes and offerings."

As a result, Christians are falling with the world into a pit of ever increasing debt. We have invested in money market funds, CDs, 401Ks, and real estate, and have foolishly neglected to cheerfully pay our tithes and sow our offerings into the kingdom of God, which is guaranteed to produce 30, 60, and even 100 fold returns (II Corinthians 9:7, Mark 4:20).

Laying the Ax to the Root

Seeing the depravity of the Church, numerous preachers and teachers have valiantly taught on prayer, tithing and against divorce. Nevertheless, their efforts have affected minimal change. Although their messages are Biblical and anointed, they have primarily ministered to the symptoms of sin, instead of laying the spiritual ax to the root of sin.

Ironically, the same prescription for sin that the prophet Malachi offered as a remedy to Israel's sins almost 2500 years ago is available to the Church today. That remedy is the fear of the Lord (Malachi 1:14, 2:5,6, 3:5).

> **Malachi 4:2 "But to you who fear My name the Sun of Righteousness shall arise with healing in His wings."**

The fear of the Lord is to hate evil (Proverbs 8:13). By the fear of the Lord we depart from evil, obey the commandments and Holy Spirit of God, and are perfected in holiness (Proverbs 16:6, Ecclesiastes 12:13, II Corinthians

114

7:1). Satan has successfully kept this fundamental spiritual truth out of many pulpits throughout America. As a result, the Holy Spirit of judgment and burning has been hindered from operating in our churches and personal lives to cleanse, purge and sanctify us that we might be revived and transformed into vessels of honor fit for the Master's use (II Timothy 2:19-21).

> Isaiah 4:3,4 "He who is left in Zion will be called holy, when the Lord has washed away the filth of the daughters of Zion by **the spirit of judgment and by the spirit of burning.**"

The Master's Prescription

The degree of healing that the Sun of Righteousness can bring to the Church in the Valley of the Sun is directly proportional to the degree to which the fear of the Lord is wrought in us. Jesus delighted Himself in the fear of the Lord (Isaiah 11:3). Since it is our goal to be conformed to the image of Christ, we should make it our aim to pursue the fear of the Lord.

The fear of the Lord is the Master's prescription for healing the Church and the world of rebellion and lawlessness. The fear of the Lord is wrought in us by the Spirit of judgment and burning through the baptism of fire (Matthew 3:11).

> II Chronicles 7:14 "**If My people** who are called by My name **will humble themselves**, and pray and seek My face, and turn from their wicked ways, then **I will** hear from heaven, and will forgive their sin and **heal their land.**"

Humility or meekness is the fruit of the Spirit that characterizes those who fear the Lord. We give the Holy Spirit access into our lives to perform this baptism of fire

115

when we humble ourselves through an absolute surrender to God. Only then can the Lord begin to spiritually revive us.

> Isaiah 57:15   "For thus says the High and Lofty One Who inhabits eternity, whose name is Holy: '**I dwell in the high and holy place, with him who has a contrite and humble spirit, to revive the spirit of the humble, and to revive the heart of the contrite ones.**'"

Our unconditional surrender to the Lord, oftentimes wrought through prayer and fasting, allows us to draw nearer to Him to seek His face. Like the prophet Isaiah, as we enter into His glorious manifest presence, our iniquities are exposed (Isaiah 6:1-6). Through the Spirit of the fear of the Lord, the grace of repentance is imparted to us, resulting in our conviction, confession and forsaking of sin (Proverbs 28:13). Personal repentance allows the Sun of Righteousness to arise in our hearts to heal and revive our spirits. Likewise, corporate repentance produces healing and revival in the Church as a whole.

Preparing the Way for the Sun

The Sun of Righteousness is sending before Him messengers to prepare the way for His rising in the Valley of the Sun.

> Malachi 3:1   "**Behold, I send My messenger, and he will prepare the way before Me. And the Lord, whom you seek, will suddenly come to his temple**, even the Messenger of the covenant, in whom you delight. Behold, He is coming, says the Lord of hosts."

Like Elijah and John the Baptist of old, modern day prophets are being sent by God to the Valley of the Sun. As these prophets preach repentance, Christian's hearts will first be turned toward our heavenly Father, and then turned toward one another in reconciliation and unity.

> Malachi 4:5,6   "Behold, **I will send you Elijah** the prophet before the coming of the great and dreadful day of the Lord.   And **he will turn the hearts of the fathers to the children, and the hearts of the children to their fathers.**"

As the message and Spirit of the fear of the Lord is welcomed in the Valley of the Sun, like the Phoenix, the Sun of Righteousness will arise suddenly in all of His glory to purify and heal the Greater Phoenician Church.

> Malachi 3:2,3   "But who can endure the day of His coming?   And who can stand when He appears? For He is like a refiner's fire and like fullers' soap. **He will sit as a refiner and a purifier of silver; He will purify the sons of Levi, and purge them as gold and silver**, that they may offer to the Lord an offering in righteousness."

After Isaiah repented and was cleansed of his iniquities in the presence of the King, the Lord commissioned him to fulfill his mission as a prophet to Judah and other surrounding nations (Isaiah 6:5-13).   Similarly, after the Church in the Valley of the Sun corporately repents and is cleansed by the Sun of Righteousness through the baptism of fire, He can then fully empower and commission us to bring healing to Phoenix's growing multitude.   The Church's revived hunger for the presence and glory of God will set in motion certain kingdom principles that will enable us to fulfill God's purposes in our city.

117

Chapter 12

Keys to Revival

Spiritual revival is necessary for the Church to fulfill Christ's great commission in the earth. Certain kingdom principles must be in operation for spiritual revival to transform, inspire and empower the Greater Phoenician Church. Only then can Christ fully work through us to transform the Valley of the Sun into a 21st century city of refuge.

Although the means by which revival is implemented in the Valley of the Sun may differ from other outpourings, the principles remain the same. Two 20th century revivals that had significant and lasting effects on the entire world were the Welsh Revival of 1904-1905 and the Azusa Street Revival of 1906-1909. References to these and other outpourings are presented to support the following keys to revival.

The Foundation of Repentance

Repentance is the foundation of revival. It is interesting to note that Jesus and John the Baptist commenced their ministries with the words, "Repent, for the kingdom of heaven is at hand!" (Matthew 3:2, 4:17). Azusa Street revivalist Frank Bartleman wrote, "I received from God early in 1905 the following keynote to revival: *'The depth of revival will be determined exactly by the depth of the spirit of repentance.'* In fact, this is the key to every true revival born of God."[1] Similarly, Welsh revivalist Evan Roberts wrote, "Every outpouring of the Spirit is preceded by earnest, agonizing intercession, accompanied by a heartbrokenness and humiliation before God. Let no one pray for revival who is not prepared for deep heart-searchings and confession of sin in his personal life. Revival in its beginnings, is a most humiliating experience."[2]

Without repentance, we remain unchanged. As we humble ourselves before the Lord, He exalts us into His Holy presence and uncovers our iniquities. We respond to His grace of repentance by confessing and forsaking our sins, which allows the Lord to baptize us in and cleanse us by the Spirit of judgment and burning (Isaiah 6:1-6).

Transforming Glory

Glory is the atmosphere of God and of revival. Our daily passionate pursuit of the Father's face through prayer, praise and worship, allows us to progressively enter deeper into His glory. As we abide in the glory of the Lord, the Spirit of the Lord transforms us into the image of Christ.

> II Corinthians 3:18   "But we all, with unveiled face, beholding as in a mirror the glory of the Lord, are being transformed into the same image from glory to glory, just as by the Spirit of the Lord."

Glory is the atmosphere wherein darkness is dispelled and the light of the knowledge of the glory of Christ is manifested. The glorious secret place of the Most High is where revelations are received, anointings are imparted, callings are confirmed, ministers are commissioned, bodies are healed, bondages are broken and prayers are answered.

A Vision from the Lord

Every revival that has brought substantial, lasting change to a society was birthed in the heart of a person or group of people that had a vision from the Lord. As was discussed in detail in Chapter 6 of this book, God first builds everything on revelation knowledge of His divine purpose. In order for us to be effectively used by God to transform the Valley of the Sun, we must first have a corporate vision from the Lord to do so. Otherwise, we are like a framing company attempting to build a house without a blueprint.

Evan Roberts, the forerunner of the Welsh revival, began praying for revival to visit Wales at age eleven. Finally, in 1904, at age 26, the young revivalist received his vision from the Lord for the Welsh Revival.

> Roberts records, "I had a vision of Wales being lifted up to heaven. We are going to see the mightiest revival that Wales has ever known and the Holy Spirit is coming just now. We must get ready. We must have a little band and go all over the country preaching." Suddenly Evan stopped and with piercing eyes he looked into his friend's face. "DO YOU BELIEVE THAT GOD CAN GIVE US 100,000 SOULS NOW?" he asked.[3]

Similarly, a great burden came upon Frank Bartleman to see the kind of revival that he had heard about in Wales, which not only changed individuals, but also changed entire cities. With this new vision, he then began to pray for an outpouring of the Spirit for Los Angeles and the whole of Southern California.[4] Little did Bartleman realize that the revival the Lord was birthing through him would impact the nations of the world.

A Burden for the Lost

As we draw nearer to the Father, we not only receive His vision but also share His burden. The heartbeat of the Father is to reconcile to Himself every lost man, woman and child. The thought of eternally losing even one person to a Christless hell breaks the heart of the Father

(John 3:16, II Peter 3:9). The Apostle Paul is an example of one who partook of the sufferings of Christ by sharing the Lord's burden for the salvation of His beloved Israel (Romans 10:1).

> Romans 9:1-3   "I tell the truth in Christ, I am not lying, my conscience also bearing me witness in the Holy Spirit, that I have great sorrow and continued grief in my heart. For I wish that I myself were accursed from Christ for my brethren, my kinsmen according to the flesh."

In every true revival born of God, the main focus of prayer is always for the lost. On the night that he received his vision for the Welsh Revival, Evan Roberts records, "I fell on my knees with my arms over the seat in front of me and tears flowed freely. I cried "Bend Me! Bend Me! Bend Me!" Now a great burden came upon me for the salvation of lost souls." From this tiny spark, practically every Christian in Wales erupted simultaneously with a burning agony for the lost.[5]

In like manner, from 1904 through 1910, missionary John "Praying" Hyde carried the Lord's burden in prayer for the lost in India. One author noted, "Hyde never seemed to lose sight of those thousands in his own district without God and without hope in the world. How he pleaded for them with sobs that showed how the depths of his soul were being stirred. 'Father, give me these souls, or I die!' was the burden of his prayers."[6]

Fervent Intercession

Jesus, who forever makes intercession for saints and sinners alike, desires every believer to partake of His sufferings through the ministry of prayer (Hebrews 7:25, Philippians 3:10). As we yoke ourselves together with Jesus in fervent, effectual intercession, the transformation of the saints and the birthing of souls into the kingdom of God is imminent (Psalm 126:5,6, James 5:16).

Galatians 4:19   "My little children, for whom I labor in birth again until Christ is formed in you."

Isaiah 66:8   "For as soon as Zion travailed, she gave birth to her children."

Usually the sacrificial intercession of a persistent few paves the way for revival. For instance, Evan Roberts earnestly prayed for revival for fifteen years before he witnessed the fruit of his labors - a united, corporate, fervent army of intercessors. Roberts reports, "It was praying that rent the heavens. The spirit of intercession was so mightily poured out that the whole congregation would take part simultaneously for hours!   The whole community was shaken. At 6 A.M. the people would be awakened by the sound of the crowds going to the early morning prayer meeting. The entire population of the town was being transformed into a praying multitude."[7]

During the Welsh Revival, Azusa's Frank Bartleman knew that the Lord was preparing intercessors not only in Wales and Los Angeles, but also throughout the nations of the world. Bartleman writes, "A great burden and cry came in my heart for a mighty revival. Many were being similarly prepared at this time in different parts of the world. The Lord was preparing to visit and deliver his people. Intercessors were the need."[8]

Sacrificing sleep and nourishment, Bartleman often spent entire nights in prayer. He records, "The spirit of prayer came more and more heavily upon us. I would lie on my bed in the daytime and roll and groan under the burden. At night I could scarcely sleep for the spirit of prayer. I fasted much, not caring for food while burdened. At one time I was in soul travail for nearly twenty-four hours without intermission. It nearly used me up. Prayer literally consumed me. I would groan all night in my sleep."[9] (Romans 8:26,27).

Unity of the Spirit

As we corporately partake of Christ's sufferings through the ministry of intercession, the glory of the Lord rises upon us (Isaiah 60:1-3). In the glorious presence of the King, our focus tends to shift toward the Prince of Peace and away from our selfish motives, religious forms and intolerant traditions that serve to cloud our vision and separate the Body of Christ.

> John 17:22 "And **the glory** which You gave Me **I have given them, that they may be one** just as We are one."

As we abide in the glory of the Lord, the bond of peace more perfectly unites the Church in and by the Holy Spirit (Ephesians 4:1-3).

As the unity of the Spirit is experienced in ever increasing measures, we will all find a growing need within ourselves to be joined with unfamiliar or estranged members of the Body. Whether doctrinal differences have separated us or denominational walls have isolated us, believers must come together as one.

Welsh revivalist Evan Roberts remarks, "One of the most significant results was that the old church prejudices were broken down. The man-made denominational barriers completely collapsed as believers and pastors of all denominations worshipped their majestic Lord together. The quarrels of local Christians were healed."[10]

In Jesus' prayer to the Father for all believers before His crucifixion, the unity of all believers can be clearly

123

identified as the key to the Church fulfilling the Lord's Great Commission.

> John 17:20,21   "I do not pray for these alone, but also for those who will believe in Me through their word; **that they all may be one**, as You, Father, are in Me, and I in You; that they all may be one in Us, **that the world may believe that You sent Me**."

Only when believers begin to truly walk together as one will the world believe in the Father's love, which was manifested through Him sending His only begotten Son, Jesus Christ, to die for the sins of all mankind.

Unity of the Faith

Although the Body of Christ has made significant strides toward New Testament corporate unity, denominational, doctrinal walls of division that separate the Body of Christ must continue to come down.

> Romans 15:5-7   "Now may the God of patience and comfort grant you to be like-minded toward one another, according to Jesus Christ, that you may with one mind and one mouth glorify the God and Father of our Lord Jesus Christ. Therefore receive one another, just as Christ also received us, to the glory of God."

Some Christians feel that they cannot fellowship with believers from other denominations because of minor doctrinal differences (Amos 3:3). However, the Apostle Paul answers this objection in his letter to the Roman church, and supports our unqualified reception of those who confess the name of our Lord and Savior Jesus Christ and hold to the major doctrines of the New Testament (Hebrews 6:1,2).

> Romans 14:1   "Receive one who is weak in the faith, but not to disputes over doubtful things."

Issues such as Bible version preference, methods of baptizing new believers, forms of prayer, and worship styles should not hinder fellowship and unity among Christians. We may not agree on every minor doctrinal issue, yet the agreeable Spirit within us is peaceable and willing to make allowances for other believers.

Commanded Blessings

The apostles who accompanied Jesus while He prayed to the Father in Gethsemane, certainly took to heart what Jesus prayed that night before His death on the cross. The book of Acts records that the apostles and disciples were continually in one accord, laying down their lives for one another in covenant love (Acts 1:14; 2:1, 44-47; 4:32-37). Because of their uncompromising obedience and commitment to walking in unity, the Lord commanded many blessings upon the early Church. The life of God, "Zoe" in the Greek language, is multiplied and released through the Church when believers commit to walking in the unity of the Spirit .

> Psalm 133:1-3   **"Behold, how good and how pleasant it is for brethren to dwell together in unity!** It is like the precious oil upon the head, running down on the beard, the beard of Aaron, running down on the edge of his garments. It is like the dew of Hermon, descending upon the mountains of Zion; **for there the Lord commanded the blessing - life forevermore."**

The anointing to promote unity, that rests upon the ministry gifts of the apostle, prophet, evangelist, pastor and teacher, must flow down to the rest of the Body. These ministry gifts, as proponents or agents of unity, are responsible to initiate and maintain unity among the brethren throughout the Body of Christ (Ephesians 4:11-13).

Endeavoring "to keep the unity of the Spirit in the bond of peace" is imperative if we ever expect to fulfill our heavenly calling (Ephesians 4:3,4). As we all walk worthy of the Lord's calling upon us by being patient and tolerant, speaking the truth in love, and humbly submitting to one another in the fear of God, we will begin to see brethren united (Ephesians 4:1,2,15; 5:21).

> Philippians 2:1,2 "Therefore, if there is any consolation in Christ, if any comfort of love, if any fellowship of the Spirit, if any affection and mercy, fulfill my joy by being like-minded, having the same love, being of one accord, of one mind."

The apostle Paul also exhorted believers to avoid those who called themselves Christians but generated strife and contention in the Body (Ephesians 4:14).

> Romans 16:17 "Now I urge you, brethren, note those who cause divisions and offenses, contrary to the doctrine which you learned, and avoid them."

Why were the apostles so committed to the unity of the Spirit, and why did they seek to maintain it at any cost as Jesus commanded?" The answer to this question is found in the Book of Acts.

Demonstrations of Power

Jesus promises us that if we come together as one in purpose, motive, spirit and faith, the world around us

126

would understand and receive of the Father's love and come to the saving knowledge of Jesus Christ (John 17:20,23). Therefore, the unity of the Spirit, manifested in our love and devotion to one another, becomes our greatest evangelistic tool (John 13:34,35, II Corinthians 3:2).

However, our testimony of love for one another is not the only effective soul-winning tool that walking in the unity of the Spirit affords us. The Lord also entrusts Spirit united believers with the gifts of the Holy Spirit, which confirm the Gospel of salvation that we preach (Mark 16:20).

> Acts 4:32,33   **"Now the multitude of those who believed were of one heart and one soul**; neither did anyone say that any of the things he possessed was his own, but they had all things in common. **And with great power the apostles gave witness to the resurrection of the Lord Jesus.** And great grace was upon them all."

> Acts 2:42,43   **"And they continued steadfastly in the apostles' doctrine and fellowship**, in the breaking of bread, and in prayers. Then fear came upon every soul, and **many wonders and signs were done through the apostles."**

The signs and wonders demonstrated by the apostles were evidence of their commitment and devotion to maintaining the unity of the Spirit among the brethren.

A Harvest of Souls

The unity of the Spirit that was present among the apostles, which brought the glory and miracle working power of God, became the proof of the salvation message they preached.

127

Acts 5:12,14 "And through the hands of the apostles many signs and wonders were done among the people. And they were all with one accord in Solomon's Porch. And **believers were increasingly added to the Lord, multitudes of both men and women.**"

Acts 2:46,47 "So continuing daily with one accord in the temple, and breaking bread from house to house, they ate their food with gladness and simplicity of heart, praising God and having favor with all the people. And **the Lord added to the church daily those who were being saved.**"

The miracles that people experienced caused them to believe in Jesus Christ, adding many to the kingdom of God (Acts 5:12-16). This same power to save lives and heal bodies is available to the Church today, if we will earnestly endeavor to walk in covenant unity with our brethren.

The Author and Finisher of our faith is also the Author of revival. Although the prescription for revival cannot be reduced to a mere formula, the kingdom principles of revival shared in this chapter are universal. They are biblical, timeless, proven and repeatable. Prophetically speaking, it is now time for the Body of Christ in the Valley of the Sun to prepare for the Lord's visitation, for indeed the Sun of Righteousness shall arise with healing in His wings to revive Greater Phoenix at the dawn of the 21st century.

Chapter 13

The Transformation of Phoenix

The Church's renewed spiritual fervor and hunger for the presence and power of the Lord should always produce in us a desire to go as lights into our world to manifest and establish the kingdom of God. For indeed, the ultimate purpose of revival in the Church is not only to draw Christians closer to the Lord, but to spiritually transform society. This concept of societal reformation is more commonly referred to as "community transformation".[1]

This book is not only intended to describe the Lord's unique prophetic prescription for reviving the Church in the Valley of the Sun, but also to set a heavenly vision before us concerning the transformation of Greater Phoenix.

City Church - From Concept to Conquest

True unity of the Spirit is not characterized merely by the absence of strife or competition among an assembled group of pastors, but by a cooperative pursuit of a common purpose or vision birthed in the heart of God. It is not crucial that all the pastors and Christian leaders in the Valley of the Sun know one another. What is important is that a common vision and purpose from God for Greater Phoenix is shared and pursued by spiritual leadership.

There are groups of pastors throughout Greater Phoenix who have a revelation of the importance of the unity of the Spirit. As a result, they meet regularly for the purpose of establishing accountable godly relationships, which is building a foundation for a Spirit united city Church. Their goal is to incur the commanded blessing of

God that will corporately empower the Church to impact Greater Phoenix for the Lord Jesus Christ (Psalm 133).

The unity of the Spirit can only be accomplished among brethren through active relationships. As pastors and leaders submit themselves and their ministries to one another in the fear of God, the Lord will promote them to higher levels of spiritual authority, resulting in greater influence for Christ in the city. Therefore, transparency among leaders is a must if the unity of the Spirit is going to be achieved in the Valley of the Sun (Ephesians 5:21, James 5:16).

Unfortunately, some pastors within our city will not meet with other pastors, erroneously thinking that they are superior to other ministers or feeling that they do not need anyone to help them fulfill their divine mission. Other Phoenician pastors are intimidated by other pastors, feeling that if they or their congregations fellowship with those from another church, they could potentially lose some of their members. Still others feel that fellowshipping and praying with other pastors and congregations is inconsequential. Many feel that if they simply build the church they are overseeing, they are doing their job.

However, the Lord wants us to impact and transform cities. Certainly one lone pastor, church, or denomination cannot conquer all the strongholds of darkness over Greater Phoenix and win the entire city to Jesus. It will take the effectual cooperation of all the churches in the Valley of the Sun to spiritually transform our city to the glory of God.

Pipe Dream or Possibility?

Without the inspiration of modern day examples of societal reformation, it is somewhat difficult to envision a spiritually transformed Phoenix. To help rescue us from this dilemma, I have highlighted cities throughout the world that have truly been spiritually and socially transformed by the power of God.

The Welsh Revival of 1904-1905 not only set ablaze the country of Wales but spread to several countries throughout the world. The Welsh Revival produced clear evidence not only of revival but also of community transformation. Crime was so diminished that the police became unemployed in many districts. Work in coal mines was hampered because the pit ponies had to be retrained to respond to workers' new "cleaned-up" commands instead of cursing.[2] Gambling and alcohol businesses lost their trade and the theaters closed down from lack of patronage. Having a reputation of being "football mad", Welsh players and fans alike virtually forsook the game, as trains that normally transported crowds to the international games were almost empty! Famous Welsh singing festivals were transformed into revival meetings, and political meetings were canceled, as parliament members abandoned themselves to revival meetings.[3]

The following accounts are present day examples of spiritually reformed societies. The late 19th century arrival of missionaries William Frederick Savage and J.H. Lorraine in Mizoram, India sparked a flame of revival that has lasted over four generations. Surrounded by Islamic Bangladesh, Buddhist Myanmar and three Hindu states, the 750,000 population of Mizoram remarkably has been transformed from a tribe of fierce, head-hunting, idol worshipping savages to a community that is nearly 95% Christian. Currently, eighty percent of the population of Mizoram attends church at least once a week, and in great contrast to the rest of India, Mizoram has no homeless, no beggars, no starvation, and 100 percent literacy.[4]

In the mid 1970's, the Guatemalan town of Almolonga was economically depressed, inebriated and full of idolatry. Burdened by poverty and fear, Almolonga's citizens sought relief through alcohol and an idol named Maximon. In their determination to fight against this darkness, a group of local intercessors began to cry out to God during evening prayer vigils. As a result, Almolonga has become one of the most thoroughly transformed communities in the world, as 90% of their citizens are evangelical Christians. In 1994, the last of four jails, that twenty years ago were overpopulated with brawlers and drunkards, was finally closed. By 1998, this Mayan town of 19,000 had over 20 evangelical churches, four of them with a membership of over 1000 people. Several distressed taverns have been converted into churches and poverty is virtually nonexistent. Now nicknamed, "America's Vegetable Garden", Almolonga's normal 60-day growing cycle on certain vegetables has been cut to 25 days. Even more remarkably, Almolonga's agricultural productivity has increased 1000 percent, increasing from four truckloads of produce per month to 40 truckloads per day. Almolonga's colossal carrots, which are larger than an average man's forearm, and cabbages, which are larger than a basketball, have drawn university researchers from all over the world.[5]

A little closer to home, the city of Hemet, California in the mid 1970's was known as a pastor's graveyard, cult haven, and methamphetamine manufacturing capital of the West Coast. After a few resident pastors committed their lives to the city of Hemet and began praying for its transformation, things began to change. By the late nineties, cult membership sunk to 0.3 percent of the population, the drug business dropped 75 percent, church attendance doubled over a 10 year period, and the school drop-out rate in just four years went from 4.7 to 0.07 percent.[6]

Some other spiritually transformed communities throughout the world are Umuofai, Nigeria; Cali, Columbia; Kiambu, Kenya; Vitoria da Conquiste, Brazil; San

Nicolas, Argentina; Modesto, California; and Pensacola, Florida.

Persevering Spiritual Leadership

George Otis, Jr., of The Sentinel Group, has performed over a dozen case studies worldwide of modern day community transformations. He found two common elements that characterized all transformed communities. The first characteristic is persevering spiritual leadership; the second is fervent, united prayer.[7]

Spiritual leaders who are bound by the Holy Spirit to complete a particular mission inevitably will face persecution and even death. For example, the life of Colombian revivalist Pastor Julio Ceasar Ruibal was sown in martyrdom in 1995, resulting in the Spirit unification of 200 pastors and a revival that has totally transformed the city of Cali from one of the most thoroughly corrupt cities in the world to a model of societal reformation.[8]

Fulfilling greater divine purposes requires an unshakable resolve to persevere despite the weight of constant opposition. For example, Noah, who was entrusted with sustaining human and animal life in the earth during the flood, endured constant ridicule as he built the ark. Similarly, Nehemiah, who under the direction of the Holy Spirit rebuilt the walls of Jerusalem, was repeatedly threatened and opposed by Sanballat and Tobiah.[9] In these last days, as a great war continues to rage in the heavenlies over the eternal destiny of millions, we should not only prepare for, but also expect great opposition from Satan.

Persistent Prayer

The second characteristic that George Otis, Jr. found to characterize all transformed communities was fervent, united prayer. Historically, spiritual breakthroughs occur when intercessors fervently and specifically petition the Lord while sharing a common vision or goal. Corporate intercession can take many different forms. For example, in Cali, Columbia, 60,000 intercessors convene every 90 days for all night prayer vigils. What is critical is not the form, but the fervency and perseverance of intercession. Unfortunately, the fervency of intercessors often begins to wane long before spiritual breakthroughs occur. This is primarily due to a lack of progressive revelation of a community's divine destiny and demonic deterrents, resulting in aimless, ineffectual prayer. In a nutshell, intercession perishes due to a lack of knowledge and vision (Hosea 4:6, Proverbs 29:18).[10]

The key to maintaining fervent intercession that yields positive results is having a continual flow of inspirational revelation. Progressive revelation can come through natural or supernatural means. One proven method of receiving revelation concerning not only the schemes of Satan but also the plans of God for a given community is commonly referred to as "spiritual mapping". Spiritual mapping utilizes historical, geographical and spiritual insight to effectively identify demonic origins and defeat them through strategic intercession. Undertaking a successful strategic prayer and spiritual mapping campaign demands that participants be intimately acquainted with their community and sincerely concerned about the eternal destiny of its inhabitants.[11]

Although this book contains many key insights into Greater Phoenix's divine destiny and demonic deterrents, it is not intended to be a comprehensive "spiritual map" of the Valley of the Sun. This book is to provide a firm foundation on which a successful spiritual mapping and strategic prayer campaign for Greater Phoenix can be solidly built. For an in-depth study on the art of spiritual mapping and strategic prayer, I recommend the book *Informed Intercession* by George Otis, Jr.

It is encouraging to know that a foundation for corporate, united, fervent intercession is being laid in the Valley of the Sun. In 1996, the BridgeBuilders International Leadership Network launched the Greater Phoenix Church Prayer Coordinators Network, which is continually training hundreds of church prayer coordinators to assist their pastors in making their local churches "houses of prayer". This church prayer coordinators network is serving as a model for other cities throughout the nation. In 1998, the BridgeBuilders International Leadership Network had also begun sponsoring "PrayerQuake", which is a multi-denominational, multi-ethnic, annual prayer event whose goal is to motivate and equip thousands of saints throughout Greater Phoenix to pray for community transformation.

Prospering Through Prophecy

In concert with spiritual mapping, an emerging, effective, proven, Bible-based means of inspiration for the entire Body of Christ is the prophetic word of the Lord. Interestingly enough, the book of Ezra not only provides us with an example of prophetic inspiration, but contains a unique prophetic message for the Church in the Valley of the Sun.

In 606 B.C., the people of Judah were taken into captivity by the Babylonians, who were overthrown by the Persians in 539 B.C. Under the Persian leadership of Cyrus, the Jews were permitted to return to Jerusalem. There were three separate exile returns to Jerusalem. The first was led by Zerubbabel, whose mission was to restore and rebuild Jerusalem's destroyed temple. Out of at least 2 million Jews that had the opportunity to return to Jerusalem, less than 3% did so. Most refused to leave the comforts of Babylon to return to the city and God of their fathers.

Under the leadership of Zerubbabel, the reconstruction of the temple began in 536 B.C. After the foundation of the temple had been laid, work on the temple ceased two years later in 534 B.C. due to Samaritan opposition. The temple was left untouched and uncompleted for fourteen years due to the selfish ambition and spiritual indifference of the Jews in Jerusalem.

However, in the year 520 B.C., the Lord sent His prophets, Haggai and Zechariah, to prophesy repentance and hope to the Jews that they might complete the temple of the Lord.

> Ezra 5:1 "Then the prophet Haggai and Zechariah, the son of Iddo, prophets, prophesied to the Jews who were in Judah and Jerusalem, in the name of the God of Israel, who was over them."

The prophetic word was the divine impetus needed to inspire Zerubbabel and Jeshua to resume rebuilding the temple.

> Ezra 5:2 "So Zerubbabel, the son of Shealtiel, and Jeshua, the son of Jehozadak, rose up and began to build the house of God which is in Jerusalem; and **the prophets of God were with them, helping them**."

Haggai's prophetic word confronted the Jews about their spiritual lethargy and awakened them to realize that they were not prospering because they were too busy building their own houses and neglecting God's house (Haggai 1:1-11).

Haggai 1:2-5, 9   "Thus speaks the Lord of hosts, saying: 'This people says, "The time has not come, the time that the Lord's house should be built."' Then the word of the Lord came by Haggai the prophet, saying, 'Is it time for you yourselves to dwell in your paneled houses, and this temple to lie in ruins?' Now therefore, thus says the Lord of hosts: 'Consider your ways! You looked for much, but indeed it came to little; and when you brought it home, I blew it away. Why?' says the Lord of hosts. 'Because of My house that is in ruins, while every one of you runs to his own house.'"

This prophetic scripture is a word in season to the Church in the Valley of the Sun. Phoenix currently has approximately one third the number of churches of other U.S. cities having similar population. With Greater Phoenix's population swelling to over 3 million people, it is sad to think that if all the churches in the area were to triple in size, we could only minister to only 17% of the entire population! Presently, if more that 5% of Greater Phoenix's population attended church, our existing churches unfortunately could not accommodate the crowds.[12]

Many Christians throughout Greater Phoenix are not prospering because they have forsaken the work of the Lord in favor of building their own kingdoms of pleasure. Corporately, we are more interested in claiming houses and cars for ourselves than claiming lost souls for Jesus. Therefore, the Lord is sending His prophets to confront complacency and a spirit of covetousness that has captivated the hearts of many believers throughout the Valley of the Sun. Our corporate response to these prophetic words will determine if we will be prepared in the natural and in the spirit for the multitudes that will flood the Valley of the Sun in the early part of the 21st century.

The prophet Zechariah encouraged Zerubbabel to resume rebuilding the temple by prophesying that the

137

monumental endeavor that he was undertaking was inspired by the Holy Spirit, Who would also empower him to complete the task (Zechariah 1-8).

> Zechariah 4:6   "This is the word of the Lord to Zerubbabel: 'Not by might, nor by power, but by My Spirit,' says the Lord of Hosts."

> Zechariah 4:9,10   "The hands of Zerubbabel have laid the foundation of this temple; his hands shall also finish it. Then you will know that the Lord of Hosts has sent me to you. For who has despised the day of small things?"

In like manner, the Lord is sending forth His prophets to exhort the Greater Phoenician Church to prepare for a great harvest of souls in the Valley of the Sun. As the Church is revived by the Spirit, a habitation in the Spirit will be built that will draw multitudes to the saving knowledge of the Lord Jesus Christ. To accommodate the growing hunger for the knowledge and presence of God, many new church facilities will have to be built.

> Ezra 6:14   "So the elders of the Jews built, and **they prospered through the prophesying of Haggai the prophet and Zechariah**, the son of Iddo. And they built and finished it (the temple), according to the commandment of the God of Israel."

The temple in Jerusalem was completed in 516 B.C., only four years after the Jews resumed work on it. Like Malachi and Zechariah, end time prophets are being divinely commissioned to the Valley of the Sun to catalyze the redemption of wasted years of inactivity and fruitlessness (Ephesians 5:16). Like Zerubbabel, if we believe and respond to the word of the Lord through His prophets, we will prosper.

II Chronicles 20:20   "Believe in the Lord your God, and you shall be established; **believe His prophets, and you shall prosper.**"

The Biblical meaning for the word "prosper" in this context means "to have a good journey". A good journey is one in which we reach our destination safely. For example, if one plans and embarks on a trip from San Diego to New York and only makes it as far as Philadelphia, the trip was not prosperous. Similarly, if we do not complete the work that the Lord has destined for us, it not only adversely affects our lives but the lives of those around us. If the Body of Christ in the Valley of the Sun heeds the prophetic word of the Lord, we corporately will safely reach our divine destination which is community transformation.

Chapter 14

The Coming Plight and Flight

Prevailing questions that probably have lingered in the hearts of many reading this book are, "Why is the Valley of the Sun the fastest growing region in America and why will there be an even greater influx of people to Phoenix in the early 21st century?" The answer to these questions is contained in Christ's redemptive purpose for Greater Phoenix.

Phoenix's divine destiny is to be a "city of refuge". People seeking refuge are attempting to escape some sort of peril. In the Old Testament, Joshua set up cities of refuge for people who unintentionally killed someone and sought sanctuary from an "avenger of blood" (Joshua 20). Although some will continue migrating to Phoenix to escape winter's freezing temperatures, many will flee to Phoenix early in the 21st century to escape the divine judgments that will be measured out on Southern California.

The Goodness and Severity of God

Although the Lord is gracious, merciful, patient, slow to wrath and quick to forgive, He also judges sin (Psalm 145:8,9, Romans 11:22).

Psalm 7:11-13 "God is a just judge, and God is angry with the wicked every day. If he does not turn back, He will sharpen His sword; He bends His bow and makes it ready. He also prepares for Himself instruments of death; He makes His arrows into fiery shafts."

The Lord's will is that none should perish but that all should come to repentance (II Peter 3:9). Therefore, in

His goodness, He extends the grace of repentance to all. However, if the goodness of the Lord that leads men to repentance is repeatedly refused, the Lord will deal severely with us in judgment, that we might then turn to Him and be saved (Romans 2:4, Colossians 3:5,6, John 3:36).

> Isaiah 26:9   "When Your judgments are in the earth, the inhabitants of the world will learn righteousness."

Throughout the Old Testament, the Lord sent His prophets to confront individuals and nations about sin. If His people would turn away and scoff at the prophetic word of repentance given by the prophet, the Lord would eventually bring judgment upon the people in the form of famine, war, earthquake, hurricane or disease (Isaiah 6:9-12; 24:5,6). For instance, Jeremiah prophesied the same word of repentance and conditional judgment to Judah for 40 years, before they finally were taken into captivity by the Babylonians.

> II Chronicles 36:15,16 "And the Lord God of their fathers sent warnings to them by His messengers, rising up early and sending them, because He had compassion on His people and on His dwelling place. But they mocked the messengers of God, despised His words, and scoffed at His prophets, until the wrath of the Lord arose against His people, till there was no remedy."

Although many people do not believe that God judges sin in the same manner today, the New Testament gives several instances of this type of judgment being measured out by the Lord on sinful and rebellious people. A classic New Testament example involved Ananias and Sapphira, who died instantly at the feet of Peter, when they lied to the Holy Spirit (Acts 5). Another example of divine judgment was wrought at the word of the Apostle Paul, who pronounced blindness upon the false prophet Bar-Jesus (Acts 13:6-12). In another instance, King Herod was struck by an angel of the Lord and died when he blasphemed and did not give glory to God (Acts 12:20-25).

The New Testament also speaks of divine conditional judgment upon city churches. In the book of Revelation, Jesus commended and instructed different city churches, and on some pronounced judgment if they would not change their ways (Revelation 2:5,16; 3:3,16).

Similarly, the Lord is bringing judgment upon the nation of America today. America has continued in her sin, killing the innocent unborn out of convenience, pursuing wanton sexual promiscuity and perversion, and loving money more than God. As a result, the Lord's judgment is manifesting in increasing measure through hurricanes, earthquakes, floods, disease, and economic upheaval. One modern day prophetic voice, David Wilkerson, explained America's condition this way:

"All around us, the Lord is pouring out His judgments on the land, and yet most Christians do not discern them! The Bible tells us God never sends judgment on a nation until he first reveals His plans to His servants, the prophets. Indeed, God always raises up men to cry out, warn and preach repentance to let people know what He is doing. But when there is no response to His warnings, God begins to judge that nation by sending what are known as corrective judgments!"[1]

The judgment of the Lord through earthquakes in this century is not foreign to America. On April 18, 1906, San Francisco, CA was devastated by a destructive earthquake in which more than 10,000 people lost their lives. Interestingly enough, in that same year, God visited the adjacent city of Los Angeles with a mighty move of His Spirit, known worldwide as the "Azusa Street Revival".

Revivalist Frank Bartleman, a catalyst of and participant in the Azusa Street Revival, attributed the earthquake to the judgment of God upon the wicked city of San Francisco.

> "I seemed to feel the wrath of God against the people and to withstand it in prayer. He showed me He was terribly grieved at their obstinacy in the face of His judgment on sin. San Francisco was a terribly wicked city."[2]

Indignant at the stubbornness of many in the face of judgment, Brother Bartleman wrote and distributed over 100,000 "Earthquake Tracts", wherein he quoted John Wesley as saying "Of all the judgments which the righteous God inflicts on sinners here, the most dreadful and destructive is an earthquake."[3] Nevertheless, Brother Bartleman found ministers and lay people alike reject the thought that God's hand was in the earthquake.

> "Nearly every pulpit in the land was working overtime to prove that God had nothing to do with earthquakes and thus allay the fears of the people. The Spirit was striving to knock at hearts with conviction, through this judgment. Even the teachers in the schools labored hard to convince the children that God was not in earthquakes. He showed me all hell was being moved to drown out His voice in the earthquake, if possible. Men had been denying His presence in the earthquake."[4]

Although many scoffed at God's judgment in the earthquake, it was effective in bringing conviction upon the people on the Pacific Coast.

"I found the earthquake had opened many hearts. The San Francisco earthquake was surely the voice of God to the people on the Pacific Coast. It was used mightily in conviction."[5]

Despite the testimony of man concerning the Lord's hand in judging sin through earthquakes, the Bible is crystal clear on the matter (Psalm 18, Isaiah 24:1,18,20, Job 9:5,6).

Isaiah 2:19   "They shall go into the holes of the rocks, and into the caves of the earth, from the terror of the Lord and the glory of His majesty, when He arises to shake the earth mightily."

Isaiah 13:11,13   "I will punish the world for its evil, and the wicked for their iniquity . . . I will shake the heavens and the earth will move out of her place, in the wrath of the Lord of hosts and in the day of His fierce anger."

Isaiah 29:6   "You will be punished by the Lord of hosts with thunder and earthquake and great noise, with storm and tempest and the flame of devouring fire."

Nahum 1:5,6   "The mountains quake before Him, the hills melt, and the earth heaves at His presence, yes, the world and all who dwell in it. Who can stand before His indignation? And who can endure the fierceness of His anger? His fury is poured out like fire, and the rocks are thrown down by Him."

Revelation 16:17,18   "Then the seventh angel poured out his bowl into the air . . . and there was a great earthquake, such a mighty and great earthquake as had not occurred since men were on the earth."

Shaking the City of Angels

Having a better Biblical perspective concerning God's judgments through earthquakes, floods, and hurricanes, we are less likely to dismiss the following prophecies and visions concerning the divine judgment of Los Angeles.

Although God may bring Los Angeles to its knees through a massive earthquake, this would not be His perfect will. The Lord, in His unfailing compassion, would much rather have people receive the goodness of His grace and repent voluntarily.

Jeremiah 18:7,8 "The instant I speak concerning a nation and concerning a kingdom, to pluck up, to pull down, and to destroy it, if that nation against whom I have spoken turns from its evil, I will relent of the disaster that I thought to bring upon it."

Through the years, proven prophetic ministries have warned Los Angeles and Southern California of divine judgment. In June 1933, William Branham, a prophet who performed undeniable miracles during The Voice of Healing movement in the late 1940's and 1950's, had seven visions concerning imminent world events, five of which have already been precisely fulfilled. In later years, Branham often spoke of a vision he had where the entire state of California west of the San Andreas Fault would be wiped out and sent into the Pacific Ocean by a massive earthquake.[6]

More recently, Morningstar prophet Rick Joyner prophesied the following in 1998:

"Judgment is about to come to Southern California because the spiritual pollution coming from there is poisoning the whole earth. I do not believe that the

145

judgment coming to the Los Angeles area has as much to do with the degree of evil as it does the ability to project evil and send it around the world. No other city in our time has caused more people to stumble than Los Angeles, mostly for what has come out of Hollywood. If a profound repentance does not come, much of the Los Angeles basin will be destroyed to the point where the ocean will lap at the base of the mountains in Pasadena. The buildings in downtown Los Angeles will sink into the earth like stones in a jar of sand when it is shaken. Repentance and intercession can remove a lot of the death and destruction, but the earthquake is still going to be a big one."[7]

Interestingly enough, "the Bible code" in two places predicts that the big earthquake will hit Los Angeles in the year 2010.[8]

The Lord in His mercy has continued to send various types of warnings to Los Angeles, many of which have been disregarded. Prophet Rick Joyner elaborates:

"We do not know at what point the Lord will relent and spare Los Angeles, but there is a delusion in much of the church now that is presuming on God's grace. There is an arrogance toward the Lord that has even permeated much of the church in Southern California. One way that it is manifested is the disregard for His warnings, and the tendency to believe that they can be handled. No one will think this after the one that is coming, even if its destructive power is reduced."[9]

Covetousness vs. Consecration

The earthquake that occurred on October 16, 1999 less than 100 miles east of Los Angeles, CA was another divine warning to the Church of the Lord's impending, conditional judgment upon Los Angeles. This particular quake contained an underlying prophetic warning to the Church in Southern California.

The epicenter of the earthquake was located in a remote, sparsely populated section of the Mohave Desert, near a town called **Joshua Tree**. The earthquake initially was publicized to be a **7** on the Richter scale and later was upgraded to a **7.1**. The night following the earthquake, the Lord prompted me to read *Joshua 7*, and to pay particular attention to verse one.

Joshua 7:1 "But the children of Israel **committed a trespass regarding the accursed things**; for Achan, of the tribe of Judah, took of the accursed things; **so the anger of the Lord burned against the children of Israel**."

Prior to Israel's conquest of Jericho, the Lord instructed Joshua and Israel to take from Jericho the silver, gold, bronze and iron as booty to be consecrated to the treasury of the Lord. However, He explicitly forbade Israel from taking things that would bring a curse on Israel (Joshua 6:18,19). Nevertheless, after the conquest of Jericho, Achan, an Israelite from the tribe of Judah, coveted and confiscated for himself a Babylonian garment, two hundred shekels of silver, and a wedge of gold weighing fifty shekels (Joshua 7:21).

The treasures that Achan took were not accursed in and of themselves, since silver and gold were among the consecrated items approved by the Lord for His treasury (Joshua 6:19). However, Achan's covetous motivation in taking these treasures for himself is what made the items accursed. If Achan would have consecrated and given the items to the Lord, he would have been blessed. Instead, His covetousness resulted in the loss of his life, the lives of

147

his family members, and the lives of the thirty-six men who died while fighting the men of Ai (Joshua 7:5,24-26).

As I prayed over this Scripture and its message to the Church, the Lord showed me that the Church in Southern California as a whole is more concerned about the wealth of the wicked than they are the eternal welfare of the wicked.

Proverbs 13:22   "The wealth of the sinner is stored up for the righteous."

The covetousness rampant throughout Southern California has largely supplanted the Church's consecration to winning the lost to Jesus Christ. As a result, the harvest is not being effectively reaped and like Achan and Israel, the Church has come under the judgment of God. If the Church in Southern California refuses to repent of her covetousness and complacency and neglects to propagate the saving gospel of Jesus Christ, an earthquake of even greater magnitude will devastate Los Angeles.

As I asked the Lord for confirmation of this prophetic word, He led me to a map of Southern California, where I found a larger town less than 15 miles east of Joshua Tree called **Twentynine Palms**, CA. I immediately went to **Psalms Twentynine** in my Bible and was shocked to find the following verse.

Psalms 29:8   "The voice of the Lord shakes the wilderness; The Lord shakes the Wilderness of Kadesh."

Kadesh, which means "consecrated", is where Korah and his company rebelled against Moses and God, and were killed in an earthquake (Numbers 16). The Wilderness of Kadesh is where the ten fearful spies persuaded Israel to remain in the wilderness for 40 years instead of

148

entering into their promised land (Numbers 13, 14). Kadesh also is where Moses in his rebellion struck the rock to bring forth water instead of speaking to the rock as God had commanded. This simple act of disobedience cost Moses the Promised Land (Numbers 20).

The Joshua Tree earthquake was the Lord's wake-up call to the Church throughout Southern California. The Church must answer this wilderness wake-up call by repenting of rebellion, complacency and covetousness, and by consecrating Herself anew to intercession and saving the lost. Only then will the judgment on Los Angeles be lessened and a great harvest of souls reaped to the glory of God.

To whom much is given, much is required (Luke 12:48). This simple Biblical principle applies not only to individuals, but also to cities and nations. The Lord has entrusted Los Angeles with a gift to affect the nations of the world. For instance, the Azusa Street revival in the early 1900s blessed countless lives not only in Southern California but throughout the world. Conversely, this gift has also been used over the past century to curse the nations of the world through Hollywood's perversity.

Biblical interpretation of names and symbols indicates that Joshua Tree literally means "**The Lord is salvation to the nations**." The Joshua Tree earthquake was also a prophetic exhortation to the Church of Southern California to stir up its gift intended to bless the nations of the world with the saving knowledge of Jesus Christ. Corporate obedience to this calling could very well determine not only the fate of Los Angeles, but more importantly, the eternal destiny of millions internationally.

The Great Escape

In 1999, as I was intensely praying for revival in the Valley of the Sun, I had a vision of a map of the Southwest portion of the United States. In the vision I saw three cities highlighted, namely Los Angeles, Phoenix and Las Vegas. During the vision two lines were drawn, one from Los Angeles to Las Vegas, and the other from Los Angeles to Phoenix. Over a period of time, the Lord related to me the following interpretation and insights concerning this vision.

As environmental judgments upon Southern California increase, a growing number of people will be moving inland to escape them. The exodus of Los Angeles and surrounding areas in the early 21st century will eventually cause an economic imbalance and crisis that will bring many souls to the feet of Jesus. Many will lose their jobs, businesses and fortunes, but will gain eternal life through Jesus Christ.

Many Christians have come to Christ as the result of personal crisis. History reveals that spiritual revival oftentimes is a product of economic upheaval. For example, in the 1857 Revival, a near socio-economic collapse jolted America away from her apathy into a national cry for spiritual reality.[10] In His great love for mankind, the Lord mercifully brings judgment, so that the lost will repent and receive Christ. Los Angeles can be saved, but only through both the goodness and severity of God.

A holy, reverential fear of the Lord will be the spiritual fruit that comes forth as a result of these judgments, providing angelic protection for the saint and salvation to the sinner.

Psalm 34:7   "The angel of the Lord encamps all around those who fear Him, and delivers them."

Jude 22,23 "And on some have compassion, making a distinction; but **others save with fear**, pulling them out of the fire, hating even the garment defiled by the flesh."

As increasing numbers of people flee Los Angeles and surrounding areas in search of refuge from environmental and economic disaster, many will be faced with starting over in a new land.

In 1999, the population of the city of Los Angeles was approximately 3.5 million; Los Angeles County was 9.6 million; and Greater Los Angeles (5 counties) was 16.3 million.[11] If only 1 percent of the Greater Los Angeles population migrates to the Valley of the Sun annually, the current growth rate of Greater Phoenix would more than double.

Good Fortune or God's Future?

The two major inland cities closest to Los Angeles are Las Vegas and Phoenix, which also are the two fastest growing major cities in the United States. Las Vegas is famous for being a year-round desert resort oasis. Las Vegas is also known for "the Strip", which is an array of luxury hotels and casinos featuring exotic entertainment and gambling, which was legalized in 1931.[12] Las Vegas promises good fortune and fun to all, but for many has become a quagmire of promiscuity, debauchery and disappointment. Unfortunately, many fleeing Southern California will attempt to drown their sorrows in the temporary pleasures of Las Vegas, but in the end will be left unfulfilled and still in search of a dream. Although there are many devout Christians appointed by the Lord to rescue lost souls there, Las Vegas is not destined to be a city of refuge.

On the other hand, Phoenix has been appointed by the Lord to be a city of refuge for the devastated souls of

151

Southern California who will be in search of God, a future and a hope (Jeremiah 29:11-13). When they flood the Valley of the Sun in the early part of the 21st century, will the Church in the Valley of the Sun be prepared to shelter these lost souls, providing sanctuaries of refuge wherein they can experience the glories of salvation?

> Isaiah 4:5,6   "Then the Lord will create above every dwelling place in Mount Zion, and above her assemblies, a cloud and smoke by day and the shining of a flaming fire by night. For over all the glory there will be a covering. And there will be a tabernacle for shade in the daytime from the heat, for **a place of refuge**, and for a shelter from storm and rain."

In the Old Testament, Joseph was sent by God to Pharaoh to prepare Egypt to be a refuge for the nations of the world in a coming time of famine. Today, the Lord has commissioned and will continue sending "Josephs" to the Valley of the Sun to prepare Greater Phoenix to be a 21st century city of refuge. Let us now discover how the Lord has already begun to spearhead this unique work here, and how we can all participate in this divine commission to the glory of God.

Chapter 15

The Phoenix Connection

Preparation is crucial to fulfilling purpose. This principle has application in every arena of life. In the natural realm, a talented athlete without the proper conditioning and training is doomed to a career of mediocrity. In the spiritual realm, someone called of God to be a great evangelist will never be commissioned by the Lord to preach his first message without the proper preparation. Similarly, Greater Phoenix will not fulfill its divine destiny as a city of refuge if we neglect to make the proper preparations.

A Time for Josephs

Joseph was called as a boy and later commissioned by the Lord to serve as prime minister of Egypt, that he might save the people of the world from certain death due to famine.

> Genesis 45:7,8 "God sent me before you to preserve a posterity for you in the earth, and to save your lives by a great deliverance. So now it was not you who sent me here, but God; and He has made me a father to Pharaoh, and lord of all his house, and a ruler throughout all the land of Egypt."

Joseph was not only appointed by God to be a spiritual leader, but also a governmental authority through which humanity could be preserved. Joseph's unique prophetic gifting enabled him not only to interpret Pharaoh's dreams but also to provide wise counsel concerning how to prepare for the imminent famine. Joseph's gift made room for him in Pharaoh's court, as he was promoted in a moment from prisoner to prime minister of Egypt.

Similarly, "Pharaohs" in the Valley of the Sun today are having divine dreams and directives to build. The Lord has impressed many to build churches, ministries, schools, hospitals, houses, businesses, apartment and office complexes in a metropolis that is already expanding at a phenomenal rate. Little do these "Pharaohs" realize that they are building a refuge for the days of famine that lie ahead. When opposition and difficulty arise to challenge their dreams, these "Pharaohs" will need "Josephs" to inspire them to continue building, not only by providing them with a sense of divine destiny but also the godly wisdom necessary to complete their mission.

Behold, These Dreamers Cometh!

God often raises up forerunners to spearhead a spiritual outpouring or the fulfillment of His divine purposes for a particular people, place or time. As we discovered in chapters 4 and 5 of this book, during Phoenix's early development, the life of William J. Murphy, also known as "The Dreamer", and the ministry of Christianna Gilchrist serve as models that characterize our city's redemptive purpose.

Among the many "Josephs" the Lord has sent and is sending to the Valley of the Sun, Pastor Tommy Barnett of Phoenix First Assembly of God is a forerunner who has practically and prophetically demonstrated the redemptive purpose of Greater Phoenix. Pastor Barnett's primary mission has been winning souls to Jesus Christ and inspiring many to "dream again" and press toward the mark for the prize of fulfilling their divine destiny to the glory of God.

Pastor Tommy Barnett has a unique apostolic gift to inspire, equip, and activate pastors, church leaders and workers on an international level in the arenas of soul winning and servant evangelism, which are key "end time" ministries that have been abandoned by some and sorely neglected by most churches. I would like to qualify this brief account of Pastor Tommy Barnett's ministry by asserting that the impartation and activation of these ministries in the Valley of the Sun is crucial in preparing Greater Phoenix to minister to the multitudes of lost and hurting people that will be flocking here from Los Angeles in the 21st century.

Sons of the Harvest

Typically, an evangelical church today will have an "altar call", inviting whatever lost sinners that happen to be in attendance to receive Christ and the gift of eternal life. This practice is Biblical, yet falls far short of the standard that Jesus set for the New Testament church. In His parable of the lost sheep, Jesus especially emphasized the active seeking out and saving of lost souls, a standard which Tommy Barnett has wholeheartedly taught and practiced throughout his ministry.

Fishing can either be a fruitless, effortless pastime, or an active labor that yields a great harvest. The families of disciples Peter and Andrew depended on them to catch fish; their well being was at stake. Jesus promised Peter and Andrew that He would make them "fishers of men", which meant to them that Jesus was depending on them to harvest lost humanity. Tommy Barnett has adopted Peter and Andrew's mentality in his own ministry and has taught thousands to be "fishers of men" by ministering to the practical physical needs and spiritual voids of lost and hurting humanity.

Matthew 4:19   "And He said to them, "Follow Me, and I will make you fishers of men."

155

Phoenix's divine connection to Los Angeles has been uniquely characterized by Pastor Barnett's divine calling to minister there. Pastor Barnett explains:

> "I dreamed of starting a ministry in Los Angeles for forty years. Despite innumerable setbacks, frustrations, and disappointments, I could never get away from that dream. I know from experience: If it's God's dream, you won't be able to let it go, and eventually it will come to pass." [1]

The product of Pastor Barnett's obedience to his L.A. dream is the Los Angeles International Church, better known as "The Dream Center", which is America's fastest growing church. Pastor Barnett and his son Matthew have given their lives to minister to the spiritual, educational, emotional and physical needs of thousands in the Los Angeles area. The transforming effect that the L.A. Dream Center is having on Los Angeles has influenced many others to raise up "dream centers" throughout America and the world.

Prophetic ministry oftentimes provides confirmation and encouragement concerning our ministerial labors. The significance of the Barnett's ministry to Los Angeles, as an international evangelistic model to the Body of Christ, is highlighted by the following prophetic insight.

The Azusa Street Revival of 1906-1909 that sparked Los Angeles and spiritually set aflame the nations of the world was birthed in prayer. Historically, Frank Bartleman has been recognized as the intercessor that led the birthing of this mighty move of the Holy Spirit. In New Testament times, the word "Bar" before a name meant "son of". For example, Bar-Jonah means "son of Jonah", Bar-Jesus means "son of Jesus", and Bartimaeus means "son of Timaeus". Within Bartleman's last name is prophetically encrypted "son of man" (**BAR**tle**MAN**). Jesus, who "ever lives to make intercession for us" instructed his disciples to pray for the Lord of the harvest to send out laborers into His harvest (Luke 10:2, Hebrews 7:25). Bartleman, whose life was consumed with intercession, took Jesus' instructions to heart. The fervent prayers of Bartleman and many like him have resulted in the sending forth of many laborers to the white harvest fields of Los Angeles (John 4:35). Truly the Barnetts, prophetically translated "son of the net" (**BARNET**t), are "fishers of men" that the Lord has sent to Los Angeles to reap a harvest of souls to the glory of God.

From Rescue to Refuge

In 1997, the Lord impressed Pastor Barnett to walk from Phoenix to Los Angeles to raise funds to refurbish the L.A. Dream Center.[2] This inspiring journey not only served to help the hurting in Los Angeles, but also was a profoundly prophetic act. In the spirit, this journey linked Phoenix to Los Angeles and characterized Phoenix's divine rescue and refuge mission to Los Angeles in the 21st century. Not only is Phoenix to help rescue from hell the unsaved multitudes in Los Angeles, but also provide refuge in the Valley of the Sun for those devastated by the environmental and economic judgments that are to come upon Southern California.

Pastor Barnett has simply been a forerunner, a "Joseph" chosen by God to help prepare Phoenix to fulfill its calling as an oasis in the coming time of famine. The Body of Christ in the Valley of the Sun would benefit from learning from this spiritual father and others like him that the Lord has so graciously planted here for such a time as this. Only then will we be properly prepared to fulfill our destiny as a 21st century city of refuge.

An Oasis in Time of Famine

From the dawning of the Hohokam Indian civilization until now, the Valley of the Sun has been earmarked by God to be a city of refuge. Although the enemy has repeatedly attempted to thwart the fulfillment of Greater Phoenix's divine destiny, the purposes of God will prevail in these last days.

We are privileged to be positioned by the Lord in the Valley of the Sun at this strategic time in history. Therefore, let us not squander this unique opportunity, but be faithful to our corporate heavenly calling. Indeed, if we, in the fear of the Lord, will humble ourselves, corporate repentance will come. In all of His glory, the Sun of Righteousness will then arise with healing in His wings to spiritually revive and unite the Church in the Valley of the Sun. Our renewed passion for Jesus will cause us to share the Lord's burden for the lost and hurting, and enable us to fervently pray for, seek out and win the lost.

When a revived 21st century Greater Phoenician Church has truly transformed the moral complexion of our city, we will then be fully prepared to minister to the multitudes of lost and hurting people who in a time of famine will be seeking an oasis. The oasis they will be seeking and finding is Christ our Refuge. In that day the Valley of the Sun will be known as "The Valley of the Son".

It is my prayer that every Christian in the Greater Phoenix area will not only read, believe and embrace the prophetic insights communicated in this book, but also be inspired to participate in the move of God that is coming to the Valley of the Son.

Endnotes

Chapter 1

1 Houk, Rose, *Hohokam - Prehistoric Cultures of the Southwest*, Tucson: Southwest Parks and Monuments Association, 1992, pg. 5.
2 Ibid, pg. 7.
3 Ibid, pg. 7.
4 *The New Encyclopedia Britannica*, 15th Edition, Chicago: Encyclopedia Britannica, Inc., 1991, Volume 29, pg. 396.
5 Houk, Rose, *Hohokam - Prehistoric Cultures of the Southwest*, Tucson: Southwest Parks and Monuments Association, 1992, pg. 7.
6 Dubé, Jim, *The City of Phoenix - A Study of Her Redemptive Value*, Phoenix: Jim Dubé, 1990, pg. 2.
7 Joyner, Rick, *A Vision of the Twelve Cities*, The Morningstar Journal, Volume 2, No. 3, Charlotte: Morningstar Publications, 1992, pgs. 55,56.
8 Houk, Rose, *Hohokam - Prehistoric Cultures of the Southwest*, Tucson: Southwest Parks and Monuments Association, 1992, pg. 9.
9 Ibid, pg. 9.

Chapter 2

1 CArizona,*Phoenix History*, http://carizona.com/phoenixhistory.html, St. Johns: CArizona, 1998, pg. 2.
2 Houk, Rose, *Hohokam - Prehistoric Cultures of the Southwest*, Tucson: Southwest Parks and Monuments Association, 1992, pg. 15.
3 Ibid, pg. 12.
4 Haury, Emil, W., *The Hohokam - Desert Farmers and Craftsmen*, Tucson: University of Arizona Press, 1976, pgs. 164-166.
5 Rane, Joel J., *A Critical Bibliography of the Hohokam*, Los Angeles: Joel J. Rane, 1993, pg. 3.

6   Dubé, Jim, *The City of Phoenix - A Study of Her Redemptive Value*, Phoenix: Jim Dubé, 1990, pg. 3.

7   Houk, Rose, *Hohokam - Prehistoric Cultures of the Southwest*, Tucson: Southwest Parks and Monuments Association, 1992, pg. 5.

8   Ibid, pg. 6.

9   Ibid, pg. 6.

10 Ibid, pg. 7.

11 Ibid, pg. 13.

12 Ibid, pg. 13.

13 Ibid, pg. 9

14 Henderson, Kathy, Hutira Johna, & Taylor, Tobi, *Layers of History - The Archaeology of Heritage Square*, Phoenix: Pueblo Grande Museum & Northland Research, Inc., 1995, pg. 21.

15 Ibid, pg. 21.

16 *The New Encyclopedia Britannica*, 15th Edition, Chicago: Encyclopedia Britannica, Inc., 1991, Volume 29, pgs. 108-117.

17 Houk, Rose, *Hohokam - Prehistoric Cultures of the Southwest*, Tucson: Southwest Parks and Monuments Association, 1992, pg. 15.

18 Ibid, pg. 15.

19 Ibid, pg. 15.

Chapter 3

1   Luckingham, Bradford, *Phoenix - The History of a Southwestern Metropolis*, Tucson: The University of Arizona Press, 1989, pg. 13.

2   Ibid, pg. 13.

3   Ibid, pgs. 14-15.

4   Ibid, pg. 15.

5   Dubé, Jim, *The City of Phoenix - A Study of Her Redemptive Value*, Phoenix: Jim Dubé, 1990, pg. 5.

6   Tucker, Suzetta, *The Bestiary - Phoenix*, http://pages.prodigy.com/Christstory/phoenix.html, Suzetta Tucker, 1997, pg. 1.

7   Phoenix Publishing,
        http://www.phoenixpublishing.com, Blaine:
        Phoenix Publishing, 1999.
8   Tucker, Suzetta, *The Bestiary - Phoenix*,
        http://pages.prodigy.com/Christstory/phoenix.html,
        Suzetta Tucker, 1997, pg. 2.
9   Dorn, John Matthew, http://www.com/itc/phoenix.html,
        Interactive Therapy Center, 1999.
10 The Center for Arizona Policy, *Covenant Marriage
        (SB-1133)*,
        http://www.cenazpol.org/issues/p5cov_mrg.html,
        1998, pg. 1.
11 Ibid, pg. 1.
12 Ibid, pg. 1.
13 Luckingham, Bradford, *Phoenix - The History of a
        Southwestern Metropolis*, Tucson: The University
        of Arizona Press, 1989, pgs. 160, 161.
14 Barker, Jeff, and Sherwood, Robbie, *Growth Spurt in
        Valley*, Phoenix: The Arizona Republic,
        November 18, 1997, pgs. A1, A10.
15 Sacks, Hal, *Phoenix Selected as Strategic Focus City,*
        The BridgeBuilder, Volume 7, Issue No. 1,
        Phoenix: BridgeBuilders International Leadership
        Network, 1999, pgs. 1, 4.
16 Arizona Ecumenical Council, *Festival of Faith 2000
        Update*, Volume 1, Spring 1999, pgs. 1, 3.

Chapter 4

1   Luckingham, Bradford, *Phoenix - The History of a
        Southwestern Metropolis*, Tucson: The University
        of Arizona Press, 1989, pg. 13.
2   Ibid, pg. 14.
3   Ibid, pg. 27.
4   Ibid, pg. 28.
5   Ibid, pg. 28.
6   The Arizona Republic, *W.J. Murphy, Pioneer and
        Builder, Dies at Age of 84*, Phoenix: The Arizona
        Republic, April 18, 1923, pg. 1.
7   Ibid, pg.2.

8   Luckingham, Bradford, *Phoenix - The History of a Southwestern Metropolis*, Tucson: The University of Arizona Press, 1989, pgs. 29, 30.

9   Ibid, pg. 29.

10 The Arizona Republic, *W.J. Murphy, Pioneer and Builder, Dies at Age of 84*, Phoenix: The Arizona Republic, April 18, 1923, pg. 2.

11 Luckingham, Bradford, *Phoenix - The History of a Southwestern Metropolis*, Tucson: The University of Arizona Press, 1989, pg. 130.

12 Arizona Weekly Gazette, *Temperance Colony of Glendale*, Glendale: Arizona Weekly Gazette, 1892.

13 Phoenix Herald, *The Glendale Colony*, Phoenix: Phoenix Herald, May 4, 1894.

14 Whatley, John, *Glendale History and Growth Traced From Early Settlers Along Salt River*, pg. 10.

15 Luckingham, Bradford, *Phoenix - The History of a Southwestern Metropolis*, Tucson: The University of Arizona Press, 1989, pgs. 130-132.

16 The Arizona Republic, *W.J. Murphy, Pioneer and Builder, Dies at Age of 84*, Phoenix: The Arizona Republic, April 18, 1923.

17 Otis, George, Jr., *Informed Intercession*, Ventura: Renew Books, 1999, pg. 60.

18 The Arizona Republic, *W.J. Murphy, Pioneer and Builder, Dies at Age of 84*, Phoenix: The Arizona Republic, April 18, 1923, pg. 3.

Chapter 5

1   Luckingham, Bradford, *Phoenix - The History of a Southwestern Metropolis*, Tucson: The University of Arizona Press, 1989, pgs. 53, 54.

2   Ibid, pg. 54.

3   Ibid, pgs. 54, 55.

4   Ibid, pg. 55.

5   Ibid, pg. 253.

6   Fiscus, Chris, *Asylum in Arizona*, Phoenix: The Arizona Republic, July 11, 1999, pg. A12.

7   Luckingham, Bradford, *Phoenix - The History of a Southwestern Metropolis*, Tucson: The University of Arizona Press, 1989, pg. 137.

8   Lockyer, Herbert, Sr., *Nelson's Illustrated Bible Dictionary*, Nashville: Thomas Nelson Publishers, 1986, pg. 658.

9   *Salt River Project*, Pamphlet Introduction, pg. 1.

10 Encyclopedia Britanica CD, *History: Modern Arizona*, Chicago: Encyclopedia Britannica, Inc., 1995.

11 *The New Encyclopedia Britannica*, 15th Edition, Chicago: Encyclopedia Britannica, Inc., 1991, Volume 12, pg. 155.

12 JPC Training & Consulting LLC, *About the Vulture Gold Mine*, http://www.jpc-training.com/vlf02.html, Minnetonka: JPC Training & Consulting LLC.

13 Luckingham, Bradford, *Phoenix - The History of a Southwestern Metropolis*, Tucson: The University of Arizona Press, 1989, pg. 138.

Chapter 7

1   Otis, George Jr., *Shadowlands & Battlefronts: Spiritual Strongholds and Emerging Breakthroughs in North America*, Lynnwood: The Sentinel Group, 1999.

2   Brinkley-Rogers, Paul, *Arizona Yields Rich Treasure of Odd Legends*, Phoenix: The Arizona Republic, January 28, 1996, pg. A13.

3   Luckingham, Bradford, *Phoenix - The History of a Southwestern Metropolis*, Tucson: The University of Arizona Press, 1989, pg. 22.

4   Groat, Joel, B., *Occultic & Masonic Influence in Early Mormonism*, Institute for Religious Research, 1996, pg. 1.

5   Ibid, pg. 1.
6   Ibid, pgs. 1-2.
7   Ibid, pg. 2.
8   Ibid, pg. 3.
9   Ibid, pg. 3.
10 Ibid, pg. 4.
11 Ibid, pg. 5.
12 Jeremiah Films, Inc., *Temple of the God Makers*, 1987.

Chapter 9

1 Luckingham, Bradford, *Phoenix - The History of a Southwestern Metropolis*, Tucson: The University of Arizona Press, 1989, pg. 8

2 Ibid, pgs. 62-66.

3 Ibid, pg. 98.

4 Ibid, pg. 34.

5 Ibid, pgs. 60, 61.

6 Ibid, pgs. 123, 124.

7 *War Relocation Authority Camps in Arizona, 1942-1946*, http://www.library.arizona.edu/images/jpamer/wraintro.html, pg. 1.

8 *Arizona Apache Wars*, http://www.geocities.com/~zybt/awars.html, pg. 1.

9 Ibid, pg. 1.

10 Ibid, pg. 3.

11 Ibid, pg. 4.

12 Ibid, pg. 5.

13 Ibid, pg. 7.

14 Johnson, Jr., G. Wesley, *Phoenix in the Twentieth Century*, Norman: University of Oklahoma Press, 1993, pgs. 53, 55.

15 Ibid, pg. 55.

16 Ibid, pg. 57, 58, 66.

17 Ibid, pg. 56, 68.

18 Mastrogiovanni, John, L., *The Spirit of the Scorpion - Conquering the Powers of Insurrection*, Kearney: Morris Publishing, 1992, pgs, 4,5.

19 Winik, Lyric Wallwork, *There's a New Generation With a Different Attitude,* New York: Parade Magazine, July 18, 1999, pgs. 6,7.

20 Wagner, Doris M., *A.D. 2000 United Prayer Track Letter*, Pasadena: Global Harvest Ministries, February, 1996, pg. 1.

21 Ibid, pg. 2.

Chapter 11

1   Phillipps, Mike and Marilyn, Marriage Ministries International, *N.A.M.E. International Marriage Conference*, Phoenix, October 1, 1999.

Chapter 12

1   Bartleman, Frank, *Azusa Street*, Plainfield: Logos International, 1980, pg.19.
2   Stewart, James A., *Invasion of Wales By the Spirit Through Evan Roberts*, Ashville: Revival Literature, pg. 21.
3   Ibid, pg. 31.
4   Bartleman, Frank, *Azusa Street*, Plainfield: Logos International, 1980, pgs. 8, 9.
5   Stewart, James A., *Invasion of Wales By the Spirit Through Evan Roberts*, Ashville: Revival Literature, pgs. 30, 31.
6   Carré, Captain E.G., *Praying Hyde*, South Plainfield: Bridge Publishing, Inc., 1982, pg. 30.
7   Stewart, James A., *Invasion of Wales By the Spirit Through Evan Roberts*, Ashville: Revival Literature, pgs. 17, 39.
8   Bartleman, Frank, *Azusa Street*, Plainfield: Logos International, 1980, pg. 8.
9   Ibid, pg. 33.
10 Stewart, James A., *Invasion of Wales By the Spirit Through Evan Roberts*, Ashville: Revival Literature, pg. 71.

Chapter 13

1   Otis, George Jr., *Informed Intercession*, Ventura: Renew Books, 1999, pg. 55.
2   Pratney, Winkie, *Revival - Principles to Change the World*, Springdale: Whitaker House, 1984, pgs. 174, 175.
3   Stewart, James A., *Invasion of Wales By the Spirit Through Evan Roberts*, Ashville: Revival Literature, pgs. 70, 71.

4   Otis, George Jr., *Informed Intercession*, Ventura:
      Renew Books, 1999, pgs. 16, 17.
5   Ibid, pgs. 18-22.
6   Ibid, pgs. 29, 32-36.
7   Ibid, pg. 56.
8   Ibid, pgs. 41, 42.
9   Ibid, pg. 57.
10 Ibid, pgs. 58, 67.
11 Ibid, pgs. 66, 67.
12 Sacks, Hal, *Phoenix Selected as Strategic Focus City,*
      The BridgeBuilder, Volume 7, Issue No. 1,
      Phoenix: BridgeBuilders International Leadership
      Network, 1999, pg. 1.

Chapter 14

1   Wilkerson, David, *The Monster Flood of '93*, Times
      Square Church Pulpit Series, 8/23/93, Lindale:
      World Challenge, 1993, pgs. 1-4.
2   Bartleman, Frank, *Azusa Street*, Plainfield: Logos
      International, 1980, pg. 50.
3   Ibid, pg. 53.
4   Ibid, pgs. 49, 50.
5   Ibid, pgs. 49, 53.
6   Strom, Andrew, *Great Healing Revivalists - How God's
      Power Came*, Andrew Strom, 1996, pg. 15.
7   Joyner, Rick, *The Morningstar Prophetic Bulletin - June
      1998*, Charlotte: Morningstar Publications, pg. 10.
8   Drosnin, Michael, *The Bible Code*, New York: Simon &
      Schuster, 1997, pgs. 141, 142.
9   Joyner, Rick, *The Morningstar Prophetic Bulletin - June
      1998*, Charlotte: Morningstar Publications, pg. 10.
10 Pratney, Winkie, *Revival - Principles to Change the
      World*, Springdale: Whitaker House, 1984,
      pg. 153.
11 California Department of Finance, Demographic
      Research Unit, *Population Trends in the Los
      Angeles Five-County Area*,
      http://www.laedc.org/stat_popul.html, pg. 1

12 *The New Encyclopedia Britannica*, 15th Edition, Chicago: Encyclopedia Britannica, Inc., 1991, Volume 7, pg. 170.

Chapter 15

1 Barnett, Tommy, *Dream Again*, Orlando: Creation House, 1998, pg. ix.
2 Ibid, pg. 70.

Bibliography

Arizona Apache Wars,
http://www.geocities.com/~zybt/awars.html.

Arizona Ecumenical Council, *Festival of Faith 2000 Update*, Volume 1, Spring 1999.

Arizona Weekly Gazette, *Temperance Colony of Glendale*, Glendale: Arizona Weekly Gazette, 1892.

Barker, Jeff, and Sherwood, Robbie, *Growth Spurt in Valley*, Phoenix: The Arizona Republic, November 18, 1997.

Barnett, Tommy, *Dream Again*, Orlando: Creation House, 1998.

Bartleman, Frank, *Azusa Street*, Plainfield: Logos International, 1980.

Brinkley-Rogers, Paul, *Arizona Yields Rich Treasure of Odd Legends*, Phoenix: The Arizona Republic, January 28, 1996.

California Department of Finance, Demographic Research Unit, *Population Trends in the Los Angeles Five-County Area*, http://www.laedc.org/stat_popul.html.

CArizona, *Phoenix History*, http://carizona.com/phoenixhistory.html, St. Johns: CArizona, 1998.

Carré, Captain E.G., *Praying Hyde*, South Plainfield: Bridge Publishing, Inc., 1982.

Drosnin, Michael, *The Bible Code*, New York: Simon & Schuster, 1997.

Dorn, John Matthew, http://www.com/itc/phoenix.html, Interactive Therapy Center, 1999.

Dubé, Jim, *The City of Phoenix - A Study of Her Redemptive Value*, Phoenix: Jim Dubé, 1990.

Encyclopedia Britanica CD, *History: Modern Arizona*, Chicago: Encyclopedia Britannica, Inc., 1995.

Fiscus, Chris, *Asylum in Arizona*, Phoenix: The Arizona Republic, July 11, 1999.

Groat, Joel, B., *Occultic & Masonic Influence in Early Mormonism*, Institute for Religious Research, 1996.

Haury, Emil, W., *The Hohokam - Desert Farmers and Craftsmen*, Tucson: University of Arizona Press, 1976.

Henderson, Kathy, Hutira Johna, and Taylor, Tobi, *Layers of History - The Archaeology of Heritage Square*, Phoenix: Pueblo Grande Museum & Northland Research, Inc., 1995.

Houk, Rose, *Hohokam - Prehistoric Cultures of the Southwest*, Tucson: Southwest Parks and Monuments Association, 1992.

Jeremiah Films, Inc., *Temple of the God Makers*, 1987.

Johnson, Jr., G. Wesley, *Phoenix in the Twentieth Century*, Norman: University of Oklahoma Press, 1993.

Johnson, Jr., G. Wesley, *Phoenix - Valley of the Sun*, Tulsa: Heritage Press, 1993.

Joyner, Rick, *A Vision of the Twelve Cities*, The Morningstar Journal, Volume 2, No. 3, Charlotte: Morningstar Publications, 1992.

Joyner, Rick, *The Morningstar Prophetic Bulletin - June 1998*, Charlotte: Morningstar Publications.

JPC Training & Consulting LLC, *About the Vulture Gold Mine*, http://www.jpc-training.com/vlf02.html, Minnetonka: JPC Training & Consulting LLC.

Lockyer, Herbert, Sr., *Nelson's Illustrated Bible Dictionary*, Nashville:Thomas Nelson Publishers, 1986.

Luckingham, Bradford, *Phoenix - The History of a Southwestern Metropolis*, Tucson: The University of Arizona Press, 1989.

Mastrogiovanni, John, L., *The Spirit of the Scorpion - Conquering the Powers of Insurrection*, Kearney: Morris Publishing, 1992.

Otis, George Jr., *Informed Intercession*, Ventura: Renew Books, 1999.

Otis, George, Jr., *Shadowlands & Battlefronts: Spiritual Strongholds and Emerging Breakthroughs in North America*, Lynnwood: The Sentinel Group, 1999.

Phillipps, Mike and Marilyn, Marriage Ministries International, *N.A.M.E. International Marriage Conference*, Phoenix, October 1, 1999.

Phoenix Herald, *The Glendale Colony*, Phoenix: Phoenix Herald, May 4, 1894.

Phoenix Publishing, http://www.phoenixpublishing.com, Blaine: Phoenix Publishing, 1999.

Pratney, Winkie, *Revival - Principles to Change the World*, Springdale: Whitaker House, 1984.

Rane, Joel J., *A Critical Bibliography of the Hohokam*, Los Angeles: Joel J. Rane, 1993.

Sacks, Hal, *Phoenix Selected as Strategic Focus City*, The BridgeBuilder, Volume 7, Issue No. 1, Phoenix: BridgeBuilders International Leadership Network, 1999.

Salt River Project, Pamphlet Introduction.

Stewart, James A., *Invasion of Wales By the Spirit Through Evan Roberts*, Ashville: Revival Literature.

Strom, Andrew, *Great Healing Revivalists - How God's Power Came*, Andrew Strom, 1996.

The Arizona Republic, *W.J. Murphy, Pioneer and Builder, Dies at Age of 84*, Phoenix: The Arizona Republic, April 18, 1923.

The Center for Arizona Policy, *Covenant Marriage (SB-1133)*, http://www.cenazpol.org/issues/ p5cov_mrg.html, 1998.

The New Encyclopedia Britannica, 15th Edition, Chicago: Encyclopedia Britannica, Inc., 1991.

Tucker, Suzetta, *The Bestiary - Phoenix*, http://pages.prodigy.com/Christstory/phoenix.html, Suzetta Tucker, 1997.

Wagner, Doris M., *A.D. 2000 United Prayer Track Letter*, Pasadena: Global Harvest Ministries, February, 1996.

War Relocation Authority Camps in Arizona, 1942-1946, http://www.library.arizona.edu/images/jpamer/ wraintro.html.

Whatley, John, *Glendale History and Growth Traced From Early Settlers Along Salt River*.

Wilkerson, David, *The Monster Flood of '93*, Times Square Church Pulpit Series, 8/23/93, Lindale: World Challenge, 1993.

Winik, Lyric Wallwork, *There's a New Generation With a Different Attitude,* New York: Parade Magazine, July 18, 1999.

Books and Booklets

The following are other books and booklets written by Robert J. Winters that are available through Restoration International Ministries and Publications, Inc.

Vessels of Honor

The Spirit of Prophecy

Repentance, Restoration, and Revival

The Joshua Generation

Reviving the Holy City

Rejected But Not Affected

Exposing the Idol of Ministry

Prophetic Seminar Syllabus

For a complete list of materials, to schedule speaking engagements or prophetic seminars, or to receive our bi-monthly newsletter, "The Restoration Register", contact Robert & Kay Winters at:

**Restoration International Ministries
and Publications, Inc.**
3914 W. Hackamore Drive
Glendale, Arizona 85310
(623) 581-0731